CY...

JACK HUGHES

Left **Makronissos Beach** Right **Kourion**

LONDON, NEW YORK,
MELBOURNE, MUNICH AND DELHI
www.dk.com

Produced by Sargasso Media Ltd,
London

Reproduced by Colourscan, Singapore
Printed and bound in China by Leo
Paper Products Ltd

First published in Great Britain in 2004
by Dorling Kindersley Limited
80 Strand, London WC2R 0RL
A Penguin Company

Copyright 2004, 2008 © Dorling
Kindersley Limited, London

Reprinted with revisions 2006, 2008

A CIP catalogue record is available from
the British Library.

ISBN: 978-1-40532-128-0

Within each Top 10 list in this book, no
hierarchy of quality or popularity is
implied. All 10 are, in the editor's
opinion, of roughly equal merit.

Contents

Cyprus's Top 10

 Key to abbreviations: Adm admission charge payable
Free no admission charge **Dis. access** disabled access

Left **Beachside café** Right **Agia Napa**

Left **Kakopetria** Right **Cypriot vineyards**

Following pages: **Kourion**

CYPRUS'S TOP 10

CYPRUS'S TOP 10

🔟 Cyprus's Highlights

Cyprus packs a remarkable array of sights and attractions into such a small space: museums and archaeological sites that span more than five millennia of history, throbbing beach resorts, medieval fortresses, age-old temples standing on empty hillsides, cool mountain forests and pretty valleys chequered with vineyards, grain fields and olive groves all complete the landscape. On an island where one can swim and ski all in the same day, this is truly a holiday paradise with something for everyone.

Nicosia Walled City

The divided city, within medieval ramparts, is full of interest. With a clutch of museums, historic buildings, a lively morning market and authentic cafés and restaurants, it merits a leisurely visit *(see pp8–9)*.

Cyprus Museum, Lefticosia (Nicosia)

This superb museum has a collection of finds from ancient and medieval sites all over the island. The display of clay figurines is just one of its fascinating items *(see pp10–11)*.

Agia Napa

This resort has a reputation as the liveliest spot in Cyprus, with great beaches, water sports and a huge number of bars, cafés and restaurants catering to every taste *(see pp12–13)*.

Pierides Foundation Museum, Larnaka

Founded by a 19th-century philanthropist to rescue Cyprus's vanishing heritage, this collection includes remarkable ancient idols and early 20th-century traditional costumes *(see pp14–15)*.

 Share your travel recommendations on traveldk.com

Ancient Amathous
It takes a little imagination to conjure up an image of Amathous in ancient times from the fragments of walls that still remain, but this hillside temple site, just a short distance from the busy coastal highway, is proof of the city's glorious past *(see pp16–17)*.

Historic Leveos (Limassol)
Narrow market streets full of food stalls and craft workshops surround the sturdy medieval castle in the heart of the old quarter. Mosques and minarets are reminders of the island's multicultural history *(see pp18–19)*.

Rizokarpason
Karpas Forest
Yialousa
Karpas Peninsula
Davlos · Galateia
Neraides
Kantara
Kantara Forest
Range
Lefkonikon
Kythrea
Agios Theodoros
Bogazi
Peristerona
Famagusta Bay
Prastio · Salamis
Askeia
Tymvou
Arsos
Ammochostas (Famagusta)
Athienou · Achna
Deryneia
Troulloi
Avgorou
Protaras
Kellia
3 Agia Napa
4 Larnaka · Cape Pyla · Cape Greko
15 — miles — 0 — km — 15
Cape Kiti
ounta nt

Kourion
The multi-tiered stone theatre of ancient Kourion is often the summer setting for concerts; when not in use it offers views over the peninsula *(see pp20–21)*.

Kato Pafos Archaeological Park
The superb mosaics that adorned the floors of lavish villas built at Pafos in its Roman Imperial heyday are now part of a UNESCO World Heritage Site. Today they are one of the island's top historical attractions *(see pp24–5)*.

Akamas Peninsula
The hillsides and headlands of the Akamas form the island's last undeveloped frontier. Here, on Cyprus's only uncrowded beaches, turtles come each year to nest *(see pp26–7)*.

Troodos Painted Churches
The plain stone walls of these old Orthodox sanctuaries, hidden in remote valleys and glens of the Troodos mountains, conceal a unique treasury of vividly coloured frescoes depicting scenes from the Old and New Testaments *(see pp22–3)*.

TOP10 Nicosia Walled City

Modern Nicosia is a cheerfully rambling sprawl that surrounds a much more picturesque inner core ringed by impressive fortifications. However, unlike many historic town centres, this carefully preserved medieval gem is still very much a living town, its streets bustling with shops, bars, restaurants and local colour. Pockets of recently restored buildings such as the Archbishop's Palace and museums reveal a glorious Byzantine past and are well worth a look. The southern part of the city is divided from the Turkish-occupied North along a line between the Pafos Gate and the Flatro (or Sibelli) Bastion.

Bastion, Famagusta Gate

The walled city is easy to explore on foot – and a nightmare to explore by any other means. Leave your car at the Tripoli Bastion car park (just south of the Pafos Gate).

• Map F3
• Tourist Office: Aristokyprou 11; Map P3; 22 67 42 64
• Ledra Lookout Point: Shacolas Building; Map P2; Open Apr–Oct: 9:30am–8pm Mon–Sun; Nov–Mar: 10am–5pm Mon–Sun; €0.85
• Agios Trypiotis: Solonos 47–9; Map P3; Open 9am–5pm daily; Free
• House of Dragoman Hadjigeorgiakis Kornesios:Patriarchou Grigoriou; Map Q3; Open 8:30am–3:30pm Mon–Fri; Adm €1.70
• Byzantine Art Museum: Archbishop Makarios III Cultural Foundation; Archbishop Kyprianos Sq; Map Q2; Open 9am–4:30pm Mon–Fri, 9am–1pm Sat; Adm €1.70

Top 10 Sights

1. Medieval Walls
2. Pafos Gate
3. Ledra Lookout Point
4. Laiki Geitonia
5. Agios Trypiotis
6. House of Dragoman Hadjigeorgiakis Kornesios
7. Byzantine Art Museum
8. Archbishop's Palace
9. Podocataro Bastion & Liberty Monument
10. Famagusta Gate

Medieval Walls
The ramparts are strengthened by 11 triangular bastions, five of which are in the southern part of Nicosia.

Pafos Gate
This gate is only 10 m (30 ft) from the Turkish zone. Inside, the Church of the Holy Cross straddles the border and its rear door, within the north zone, is always sealed.

Ledra Lookout Point
For a panoramic view of the walled city *(above)*, head for the lookout point on the 11th floor of the Shacolas Building.

Laiki Geitonia
This section of the walled city has been restored into a pedestrianized area with cafés and craft shops *(below)*. It makes a pleasant place to stop and rest your feet during a tour of the rest of the old town.

Nicosia is also known as Lefkosia in Greek and Lefkosa in Turkish

Agios Trypiotis
Built by Archbishop Germanos II in 1695, this church *(above)* is a well preserved example of the Franco-Byzantine style, merging influences from eastern and western architecture.

Map of the Walled City

Podocataro Bastion & Liberty Monument
One of the walled city's enclaves of greenery surrounds the bombastic monument celebrating independence from Britain *(left)*, unveiled in 1973.

Famagusta Gate
The Famagusta Gate *(above)* has been restored and now houses the city's Municipal Cultural Centre, with a changing schedule of exhibitions.

House of Dragoman Hadjigeorgiakis Kornesios
Inside the former home of the dragoman (mediator between Greeks and Turks) is one room furnished as it would have been in the 18th century.

Byzantine Art Museum
Pride of place in the museum is given to the Kanakaria mosaics. Dating from the 6th century, these early Christian works illustrate saints and the Apostles.

Archbishop's Palace
Built in 1960, the "new" Archbishop's Palace *(below)* mimics the Byzantine style of its predecessor. It houses the Ethnographic Museum.

History of Nicosia
The site on which Nicosia stands was occupied as early as the 3rd century BC, and later settled by Romans, Byzantines and the Knights Templar. As the capital of the Lusignan dynasty *(see p28)* it was one of the most opulent cities in Christendom. After the Ottoman conquest of 1570, its importance declined, although it continued to be the seat of Turkish governors. In 1974 the city was divided between north and south.

 Crossing from southern to northern Nicosia is permitted. If staying overnight, keep hotel receipts to show at the checkpoint. **See p117**

Cyprus Museum, Nicosia

The Cyprus Museum is world-class in every way, with a treasury of millennia-old finds, from the earliest Stone Age and Bronze Age civilizations through to the remnants of the great Christian Byzantine Empire, laid out in a way that brings the island's unique heritage back to life. Housed in a gracious historic building, the museum also benefits from its compact size and lack of crowds, making for a leisurely visit. If you're interested in the ancient world everything in the collection is worth seeing but, above all, don't miss the wonderful collection of ancient terracotta warriors and charioteers – some the size of toy soldiers, others as large as life – who gaze at you in Room 3 and seem almost eerily poised to step from their display to conquer the island once again.

Cyprus Museum façade

🍴 After visiting the museum, cross the road to the Municipal Gardens for a cool drink at the shaded outdoor café.

✪ If you visit on a Sunday morning, you'll find a colourful outdoor market close by, run by expatriate Filipinos and Sri Lankans.

• Leoforos Mouseiou 1
• Map N2
• 228 65864
• Open 9am–5pm Mon–Sat, 10am–1pm Sun
• Adm €3.40

Top 10 Exhibits

1 Neolithic Artifacts
2 Mycenaean Bronze and Pottery
3 Terracotta Warriors
4 Statue of Zeus
5 Statue of Septimius Severus
6 Enkomi Treasures
7 Pit and Chamber Tombs
8 Royal Tombs
9 Leda and the Swan
10 Lambousa Treasure

Neolithic Artifacts

Early Cypriots were Neolithic tool-users whose flint blades and implements are on display as you enter the museum. The collection also includes ornaments of shell and obsidian.

Mycenaean Bronze and Pottery

Ceramics and wine bowls *(above)* made by Mycenaean settlers are the main exhibits here, but the most striking item is a gold-inlaid bowl discovered at Enkomi.

Terracotta Warriors

An amazing army of terracotta votive figurines *(below)* discovered at the shrine at Agia Irini and dating from the 7th and 6th centuries BC. More than 2,000 were found at the site.

Statue of Zeus

Poised to hurl a thunderbolt, a marble statue of Zeus dominates Room 5. The room also houses a collection of Classical and Hellenistic statues, including one of Aphrodite from the 1st century AD.

Enkomi Treasures

The enigmatic bronze "horned god" statue (left), together with a splendid bowl stand decorated with animal figures, are the highlights of this room full of finds from the Enkomi site.

Key to Floorplan

Ground Floor

Leda and the Swan

The colourful mosaic (below), made from red, ochre, black and white tesserae (tiles), depicts the myth of Leda and the Swan and was found in one of the Hellenistic villas at Palea Pafos.

Entrance

Pit and Chamber Tombs

This eerie room recreates secret stone tombs from different eras, discovered at sites all over the island.

Royal Tombs

Ivory carvings of mythological beasts (below) once adorned one of the thrones in this collection of finds from the Royal Tombs at Salamis.

Lambousa Treasure

The superb gold and silver jewellery, plates and chalices displayed around the Leda mosaic date from the 6th century AD and were found at Lambousa in northern Cyprus.

Tomb Raiders

Tomb raiders have plundered the island's archaeological sites for centuries. The British Museum in London and the Metropolitan Museum in New York acquired some of the Lambousa treasures legitimately, but several of the finds from Enkomi were sadly stolen to be sold to antiques dealers in Europe and the rest of the world, and many other finds have vanished without trace.

Statue of Septimius Severus

The glowering, naked bronze figure of the 2nd century AD Roman emperor (above) is one of the world's most impressive relics of ancient Rome.

ᴛᴏᴘ10 Agia Napa

Agia Napa has the best beaches in Cyprus and the best nightlife in the eastern Mediterranean – so it's no surprise that this lively but laid-back resort has become a hedonistic legend in its own time, with a raucous and some-what infamous youthful clientele. Yet Agia Napa still retains some of the flavour of a typical Cypriot fishing port to charm visitors during the day. There's plenty for families too, and the long sandy beaches that stretch either side of the resort mean there's still room to escape the crowds.

DJ, Nissi Beach

✪ The best way to explore Agia Napa's beaches is to rent a moped or motor bike – but obey basic safety rules, such as wearing a helmet. Bicycles can also be rented by the day. Both can be hired from the many travel agencies and tour offices around the resort.

• Map J4
• Agia Napa Monastery: Agia Napa Square; Open daily; Free
• Waterworld: Agia Thekla 18 23 72 44 44; Open Easter–Nov: 10am–6pm daily; Adm
• Makronissos Tombs: Open daily; Free
• Famagusta Gulf Viewpoint: Kennedy, Protaras; 23 74 12 54; Open daily; Free

Top 10 Sights

1. Agia Napa Square
2. Agia Napa Monastery
3. Limnaki Harbour
4. Waterworld
5. Nissi Beach
6. Makronissos Beach
7. Makronissos Tombs
8. Potamos Liopetriou
9. Famagusta Gulf Viewpoint
10. Cape Greco

Agia Napa Square
This is the heart of the town, surrounded by trendy bars and cafés *(above)*. For most visitors it's where the evening starts – and ends.

Agia Napa Monastery
This beautiful medieval monastery is surrounded by massive defensive walls. There is an eight-sided fountain *(below)* in the middle of a cloistered courtyard, entered via an arched gateway.

Limnaki Harbour
Working fishing boats bob on the water alongside private yachts and large day-cruise ships in Agia Napa's old fishing harbour *(above)* – a little enclave of pre-tourism Cyprus, on a headland between two long sandy beaches, and a respite from the town's brashness.

Waterworld
This award-winning fun park offers wild, wet thrills for all ages, with various pools, water slides and roller-coaster rides. There's a shallow pool for toddlers, as well as two restaurants, a bar and a gift shop *(see p69).*

➡ *In the evening there is a market on Agia Napa Square selling jewellery and beachwear*

Nissi Beach
About 2 km (1.5 miles) west of the town centre this lovely long stretch of white sand *(above)* is one of the island's busiest and liveliest beaches in high season.

Map of Agia Napa district

Famagusta Gulf Viewpoint
In the village of Deryneia, 3 km (2 miles) north of Agia Napa centre, you can look across the "Green Line" to the ghost town of Famagusta, a deserted no-man's-land ever since the Turkish occupation of 1974.

Cape Greco
This headland *(above)* is the south-eastern tip of Cyprus. The view is a little spoilt by radio masts, but the clear water offers some of the best snorkelling in the area.

Makronissos Beach
Makronissos, also known as Golden Sands, is a long sandy stretch 1 km (half a mile) west of Nissi (and linked to it by a walkway and cycle path). It has a sweep of fine sand and plenty of watersports options.

Makronissos Tombs
Just inland from the Makronissos Beach, the Makronissos Tombs are funeral chambers that were cut into the rock during the time of Roman occupation.

Potamos Liopetriou
About 3 km (2 miles) west of Makronissos is this little fishing port and beach *(below)*, overlooked by the crumbling walls of a medieval watchtower.

Mystery Icon
In the 16th century a hunter's dog led him to a spring in the woods where he found a sacred icon of the Virgin that had been lost 700 years earlier. The spring was thus believed to have healing powers and the monastery of Agia Napa was built on the site. Soon after, Cyprus fell to the Turks and the Venetian monks fled, but villagers continued to use the church.

For nightlife in Agia Napa **See pp77**

🔟 Pierides Foundation Museum, Larnaka

This eclectic collection, which spans the ancient history of the island from prehistoric times through the Roman and Byzantine empires to the Middle Ages, is the oldest private museum in Cyprus and is still run by the Pierides family who established it in the 19th century. The displays of local crafts and costumes are among the best on the island. The museum has four rooms, together with exhibits in the entrance hall and corridors.

Museum façade

🍴 **For a cold drink or meal after visiting the museum, cross Zenonos Kitieos Street and walk east to Leoforos Athinon, where you will find a plethora of open-air tavernas and cafés with a view of the harbour.**

• Zenonos Kitieos 4
• Map M5
• 248 14555
• Open 9am–4pm Mon–Thu, 9am–1pm Fri–Sat
• Adm €1.70

Top 10 Exhibits

1. "Howling Man"
2. Attic Ceramics
3. Terracotta Figurines
4. The Roman Collection
5. Pomos Heads
6. Medieval Corridor
7. Archaic Pottery
8. Byzantine & Medieval Ceramics
9. Folklore Wing
10. Michael Kashalos Collection

Attic Ceramics
These painted pots *(right)* and bowls from mainland Greece are evidence of trade between ancient Cyprus and the Hellenic world. They depict Theseus and other mythical characters. Room 2.

Terracotta Figurines
The earthenware figures in this display represent actors performing the comedies written by Classical Greek playwrights in the 4th and 5th centuries BC. Room 2, Case 3.

"Howling Man"
This 5,000-year-old terracotta figure *(above)* is the largest and most striking relic yet found from the Chalcolithic era, when the island was first settled by humankind. Liquid poured into his gaping mouth (which gives the figure its name) flows down and emerges from his penis. Room 1, Case 1.

The Roman Collection
Almost 400 pieces of delicate Roman glassware *(below)* adorn the walls and display cabinets of Room 4.

Pomos Heads

These small carved limestone and terracotta heads and figures, found at Pomos on the northwest coast of Cyprus, date from both Greek and Roman times. Among the figures is a small bust of the Roman emperor Nero as a young man. Room 2.

Archaic Pottery

Finds from Margi and Kotsioitis, near Nicosia, include vases and other objects of red and black polished ware from the early Bronze Age (2500–1900 BC). There is also a terracotta idol representing a child in a cradle, and a striking earthenware figurine of the fertility goddess Astarte *(right)*. Room 1, Cases 2–4.

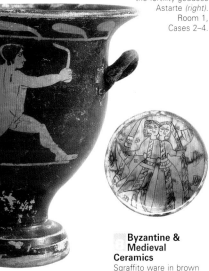

Medieval Corridor

Fascinating charts and maps *(below)*, crusader coats of arms, and ferocious Ottoman scimitars and daggers are displayed in the main corridor of the museum.

Byzantine & Medieval Ceramics

Sgraffito ware in brown and green glaze, etched with images of animals, birds, warriors, courting couples and a variety of mythical creatures *(above)* are the highlight of this collection. There are also some Byzantine icons. Room 3.

Folklore Wing

This section of the museum contains colourful traditional embroidery, antique lace, silver and amber jewellery, tools, utensils and fine antique furniture.

Michael Kashalos Collection

Michael Kashalos (1885–1974) was a self-taught painter whose depictions of Cypriot life, exhibited in the folklore wing, span more than six decades of the 20th century. Kashalos was tragically killed during the Turkish invasion of 1974.

Dimitrios Pierides

Like Greece, Egypt and other countries rich in relics of ancient civilizations, early 19th-century Cyprus was a magnet for private collectors of antiquities, as well as for looters who had a profitable trade selling artifacts to foreign museums. Dimitrios Pierides (1811–95), a wealthy merchant and financier, began his private collection in 1839, in an attempt to rescue what he could from the tomb raiders and keep the treasures in Cyprus. His descendants have continued his work, and the collection now contains some 2,500 objects.

🔟 Ancient Amathous

The foundations of ancient temples, city walls and Byzantine churches mark this evocative hillside archaeological site just outside Limassol. Founded more than 3,000 years ago, Amathous was rediscovered during the 19th century, but archaeologists continue to uncover new finds here every year. Once on the waterfront, Amathous's harbour silted up centuries ago and the site is now some distance from the sea.

Ancient city walls

⏱ To cool off after walking around the site, head for the sea at Agios Georgios Alamanou. The beach is pebbly, but the water is clean and there's a good, basic taverna, the Paraliako Kentro (996 24376).

• Coast road, 12 km (7.5 miles) east of Limassol
• Map E6
• Open 9am–6pm daily (until 7:30pm Jun–Aug)
• Adm €1.70

Top 10 Sights

1. Gymnasium
2. Church of the Port
3. Acropolis
4. Agora
5. Aqueduct
6. Roman Baths
7. Hellenistic Houses
8. Necropolis
9. Shrine of Agia Varvara
10. Medieval Mosaics

Gymnasium
Just within the entrance to the site, stone columns mark the site of the Hellenistic gymnasium, where the city's athletes trained and competed.

Church of the Port
To the left of the entrance are the foundations of a very early Christian basilica *(above)*, dating from the 5th century AD.

Acropolis
Parts of the ramparts which defended this low hilltop at the heart of the city survive *(right)*, along with the foundations of a Byzantine basilica and the remains of a temple dedicated to Aphrodite.

Agora
This expanse of worn limestone slabs *(above)* was the central gathering space and focus of the ancient city, and its size is an indicator of Amathous's importance during its hey-day. Some of the columns that surrounded the square have been rebuilt.

Aqueduct
The aqueduct and an advanced system of mains and sluices supplied the whole of ancient Amathous and its citizens with fresh water. The fascinating remains can still be seen at the northwest (upper) corner of the Agora.

Necropolis
The Necropolis, or Roman cemetery *(left)*, is on the opposite bank of the small Amathous river from the main site. Tombs were cut into the rock, and some of them were re-used centuries later during the Christian Byzantine era.

Chapel of Agia Varvara
The walls of this chapel *(below)* are decorated with frescoes of saints and martyrs, blackened with the smoke of centuries of votive candles.

Medieval Mosaics
Next to the chapel of Agia Varvara, seek out the mosaic floors of the medieval monastery which once stood here. Agia Varvara (St Barbara) is still revered by Greek Orthodox worshippers.

Roman Baths
Between the agora and the original harbour site, geometric mosaics of black and white pebbles were created as the floor of the Roman baths *(below)*.

Hellenistic Houses
Excavations continue to take place along this steep, stepped street which is lined with the walls and foundations of Hellenistic houses and shops *(above)*, and new discoveries are regularly being made.

History of Amathous
Named after the legendary prince Amathous (or, according to another legend, after Amathousa, mother of a king of Pafos), this ancient seaport flourished from as early as the 10th century BC until the 7th century AD. Raided repeatedly by Saracen corsairs, its harbour soon fell into disuse, and its end came in 1191, when it was sacked by the crusading English King Richard Coeur de Lion (the Lionheart).

TOP 10 Historic Limassol

This colourful harbour town is Cyprus's second-largest city, but at its historic heart it is a kaleidoscope of architecture, packed with reminders of the island's chequered and multicultural past, from the Crusaders through to the Venetian and Ottoman eras, to the present day. The town's museums are also a fine starting point to discover the historical background of the island. Around Limassol's medieval core the streets are lively and bustling and authentically Cypriot in character. The best way to explore the historic heart is on foot, and there are plenty of tranquil corners, including the lovely Municipal Gardens, when you want to take a break.

Limassol Harbour

🕐 Don't miss the great view of the town and its surroundings from the roof terrace of the castle.

- Map D6
- Tourist Office: Spirou Araouzou 130; 253 62756
- Limassol Castle and Medieval Museum: off Irinis; 253 05419; Open 9am–5pm Mon–Sat, 10am–1pm Sun; Adm €3.40
- Limassol Archaeological Museum: Kanningos and Vironos; 253 05157; Open 9am–5pm Mon–Fri, 10am–1pm Sat; Adm €1.70
- Municipal Folk Art Museum: Agiou Andreou; 253 62303; Open Jun–Sep: 8:30am–1:30pm, 4–6:30pm Mon–Fri (closed Thu pm); Oct–May: 3–5:30pm Mon–Fri (closed Thu pm); Adm €0.85
- Cami Kabir: Open 9am–4pm daily (closed to women and at prayer times); Free

Top 10 Sights

1. Fishermen's Harbour
2. Limassol Castle
3. Cyprus Medieval Museum
4. Cami Kabir
5. Lanitis Carob Mill Complex
6. Market Streets
7. Agia Napa Cathedral
8. Municipal Folk Art Museum
9. Limassol Archaeological Museum
10. Municipal Gardens

Fishermen's Harbour

The little wooden boats that moor here are a reminder that, before the tourism boom, Limassol was just a fishing port. The cruisers in the neighbouring marina show how things have changed.

Limassol Castle

This sturdy little stronghold *(above)* was built by the Lusignan princes on foundations erected by the Byzantines. Later Venetian, Ottoman and British occupiers strengthened its defences.

Cyprus Medieval Museum

Inside Limassol Castle this museum houses a collection of armour from the days of the Lusignans, beautiful Byzantine silverware, icons and pottery.

Cami Kabir

The graceful minaret of the city's largest mosque *(right)* is a Limassol landmark. The mosque is still used by the handful of Turkish Cypriots resident in the city, and by visitors from the Middle East.

Lanitis Carob Mill Complex

The former carob mill behind the castle is a stunning collection of vast buildings that have been tastefully converted into a trendy, multi-use complex. Examples of traditional machinery used in the mill sit among cafés, restaurants, an exhibition space and a micro-brewery.

Map of Historic Limassol

Limassol Archaeological Museum

A combination of Bronze Age pottery *(left)*, Roman glassware, gold and jewels from the Classical era and various other finds, including terracotta statuettes and votive offerings, make this museum worth a visit.

Municipal Gardens

The carefully maintained shrubs, flowerbeds and trees of the Municipal Gardens *(above)* are the venue of the annual September Wine Festival. The rest of the year this is a quieter spot. It is also home to a mini-zoo.

Market Streets

The oldest part of the city, around the castle and the Cami Kabir mosque, is gradually being smartened up. Several streets are lined with market stalls, piled with farm produce and seafood or displaying attractive traditional crafts.

Agia Napa Cathedral

On the fringes of Limassol's old quarter, the cathedral of Agia Napa *(above)*, with its twin towers and dome, is an example of Orthodox religious architecture at its florid and grandiloquent best.

Municipal Folk Art Museum

Housed in an old merchant's mansion *(left)* is a glorious clutter of farm tools, household utensils, silver necklaces and bangles, and traditional village costumes.

Richard and Berengaria

Princess Berengaria of Navarre was on her way to meet her betrothed, the English King Richard the Lionheart, in Palestine when her ship was forced to take shelter in Limassol. The city was then ruled by the Byzantine prince Isaac Komnenos, who refused Berengaria food and water. In revenge Richard landed with his army, married Berengaria, and briskly defeated Isaac to claim Cyprus for himself.

⌂10 Kourion

Looking out over the Mediterranean from its cliff top, Kourion is the most spectacularly located ancient site in Cyprus. First settled by the fierce Mycenaeans, the city reached its apogee in Roman times, as evidenced by remnants of the empire such as its great stadium, theatre and lavish public baths. As in many of Cyprus's greatest ancient cities, the cults of Aphrodite and Apollo thrived here, and both of these Hellenistic deities have shrines here. Wandering through Kourion's ruins, it is not hard to imagine the city as it must once have been: one of the jewels of Rome's eastern possessions, until its destruction by an earthquake in 365 AD.

Sanctuary of Apollo Hylates

🌐 About 3 km (1.5 miles) from the Kourion site is the village of Episkopi where there are several restaurants for a lunch break.

🕐 Visit Kourion early in the day, before the numerous escorted tour groups arrive.

• 19 km (12 miles) west of Limassol
• Map C6
• 259 34250
• Open Jun–Aug: 8am–7:30pm daily; Apr–May & Sep–Oct: 8am–6pm daily; Nov–Mar: 8am–5pm daily
• Adm €1.70
• Sanctuary of Apollo Hylates: 3 km (1.5 miles) west of Kourion; 259 91049; Open Jun–Aug: 9am–7:30pm daily; Apr–May & Sep–Oct: 9am–6pm daily; Nov–Mar: 9am–5pm daily; Adm €1.70

Top 10 Sights

1. Roman Theatre
2. Roman Baths
3. Roman Agora & Nymphaeum
4. House of the Gladiators
5. House of Achilles
6. Roman Stadium
7. Sanctuary of Apollo Hylates
8. Temple of Apollo
9. Treasury of Apollo
10. Circular Monument

Roman Theatre
Completely restored, the theatre *(right)*, with its columns and tiers of seats, is a summer venue for a range of performances, from jazz and classical music to theatrical drama.

Roman Baths

Splendid mosaics dating from the Christian era depicting fish, birds and flowers decorate the floors of the Roman baths and the adjoining villa of Eustolios. Also visible is the highly sophisticated hypocaust – underfloor heating – system *(above)*.

Roman Agora & Nymphaeum
Graceful 2nd century AD pillars of the Roman agora (marketplace) and the nymphaeum, (originally a public bathing place) can still be seen.

House of the Gladiators
This Roman villa *(below)* is named after its mosaics of gladiators in armed combat who fought in the arena.

 For more ancient sites in Cyprus See p31

House of Achilles
Next to the House of the Gladiators, this villa had a striking floor mosaic of Odysseus and Achilles, the Greek heroes of Homer's saga of the Trojan War, and of the rape of the youth Ganymede by the god Zeus.

Roman Stadium
This hillside stadium, discovered by archaeologists in 1939, could seat up to 6,000 spectators. It fell into disuse after Kourion was abandoned in the 5th century AD.

Map of Kourion area

Treasury of Apollo
Close to the Temple of Apollo is the sacred Treasury where priests made votive offerings to the god Apollo. Next to it are the remnants of a shrine dating from the 8th century BC.

Circular Monument
Ritual processions and sacred dances were held around the holy trees planted in seven rock pits surrounded by this circular mosaic pavement (above). The monument is unique in Cyprus but similar ones have been found in other parts of the world.

Sanctuary of Apollo Hylates
Standing above and to the west of Kourion, this complex of temples and shrines (below) was sacred to the sun-god Apollo. Many of its ancient walls and columns have been re-erected.

Temple of Apollo
This small temple, with its simple Doric columns (above), was one of the most sacred shrines of ancient Cyprus. The penalty for touching its altar was to be hurled from the nearby cliffs into the sea.

Greek Deities
Along with Aphrodite, who is said to have come ashore on the island, the sun-god Apollo is the Greek deity most associated with Cyprus. His cult took hold in the Hellenistic era – a fusion of Greek and Roman culture and religion. However, when Christianity came to Cyprus many of his sacred sites were taken over as places of worship.

⟨10⟩ Troodos Painted Churches

At first sight, it is hard to believe that these unassuming little stone buildings conceal such glories behind their mossy walls. Yet the isolated Troodos churches are the guardians of a unique treasury of Byzantine religious art and some of the most superb early Christian frescoes in the world. Since being given UNESCO World Heritage status in the 1980s many have been restored – although those that remain beneath a centuries-old patina are in some ways more moving and interesting.

Panagia tou Moutoulla

🗘 Plan your tour of the Troodos churches in advance. Local tourist offices may be able to help you by phoning to arrange for the caretaker to be on hand when you arrive. Unless you have a four-wheel drive vehicle, don't be tempted to take short cuts on forest tracks through the Troodos area – stick to the main roads.

• Agios Ioannis Lampadistis: Map C4; Open May–Oct: 8am–1pm, 2–6pm Tue–Sun; Nov–Apr: 8am–1pm, 2–4pm Tue–Sun; Adm CY£0.50
• Other churches are open on request. Keys are held by local caretakers, whose address and telephone number are posted at each church.

Top 10 Churches

1. Agios Ioannis Lampadistis
2. Panagia tou Moutoulla
3. Archangelos Michael
4. Agios Nikolaos tis Stegis
5. Panagia Podithou
6. Panagia Forviotissa
7. Stavros tou Agiasmati
8. Panagia tou Araka
9. Agios Sotiros tou Sotirou
10. Timiou Stavrou

Agios Ioannis Lampadistis
Three churches stand within the walls of this ancient monastery *(above)*. Inside is a superb *Pantokrator* (Christ) painting in the dome.

Panagia tou Moutoulla
One of the oldest of the Troodos churches (1279), this chapel of the Virgin has rare frescoes of St George and St Christopher – both arrayed for battle in Byzantine armour – and of the Virgin and the infant Christ. As yet unrestored, they are redolent of history.

Archangelos Michael
The frescoes of this village church *(below)*, dating from 1474, are more lively than some of their rivals. Their colours were brightened by restoration in 1980 and include a range of Gospel and Old Testament scenes.

Agios Nikolaos tis Stegis

One of the oldest of the island's churches to be dedicated to St Nicholas, this former monastery chapel features some beautiful frescoes from the 11th to the 15th centuries *(right)*.

Panagia Forviotissa

The Church of Our Lady of the Meadows stands on its own on a wooded hillside. The interior boasts a 12th-century nave and frescoes painted between then and the early 16th century, restored in the 1960s.

Stavros tou Agiasmati

Cleaned and restored to their pristine colours, the frescoes of this 15th-century church are by the religious painter Philippos Goul. The most striking, decorating the full round of the ceiling, are scenes from the Gospels, including The Last Supper, the baptism of Christ *(below left)* and the Assumption of the Virgin Mary.

Panagia tou Araka

The serene, rather melancholy portrait of Christ *Pantokrator*, dating from 1192, that adorns the dome of this church is superbly preserved. It is surrounded by brightly coloured fresco portraits of the twelve Old Testament prophets *(centre)* and, in the apse, the twelve Church Fathers.

Panagia Podithou

Dramatic depictions of the Crucifixion and the Virgin are the most striking feature of this small 16th-century church, surrounded by fields and woodland.

Agios Sotiros tou Sotirou

The main highlight of this tiny and isolated chapel is a series of wall paintings showing scenes from the life of Christ, painted in the early 16th century.

Map of Troodos Church Sites

Timiou Stavrou (Holy Cross)

This small 14th-century church *(above)* was restored in 1995 and has a unique icon of Christ flanked by the Virgin Mary and John the Baptist. Fine wall paintings blend Byzantine Orthodox and Venetian Catholic influences.

Philippos Goul

The finest frescoes in the Troodos churches are the work of the late 15th-century icon painter Philippos (or Philip) Goul. His speciality was the depiction of Old Testament prophets and events, as well as the all-seeing Christ *Pantokrator* (the Almighty). Many Troodos churches lack the domed roof typical of Greek Orthodox places of worship, and painters such as Goul and his apprentices had to adapt their style to suit the unique architecture of sloping roofs and walls.

Kato Pafos Archaeological Park

The most accessible, exciting and inspiring archaeological site on the island, the ruins at Kato Pafos were first unearthed as recently as 1962, shedding dramatic new light on Cyprus under the Roman Empire. Now a UNESCO World Heritage Site, the remains discovered here span more than 2,000 years. The lavish mosaics found on the floors of four Roman villas indicate that this was a place of ostentatious wealth in its glory days. Some display saucy scenes of deities and mortals carousing – an indication, perhaps, that Cyprus was as much a pleasure seeker's island then as it is now.

Mosaic, House of Aion

🌊 Bring plenty of bottled water with you as there are no refreshment facilities on the site.

🚗 There's a large, free car park on the inland side of Apostolou Pavlou Street, directly opposite the harbour.

For a panoramic view, climb to the roof of the miniature Turkish castle which guards the harbour.

• Map A5
• 263 06217
• Open Sep–May: 8am–5pm daily; Jun–Aug: 8am–7:30pm daily
• Adm €3.40

Top 10 Sights

1. House of Aion
2. Villa of Theseus
3. House of Orpheus
4. House of Dionysus
5. Roman Odeon
6. Asklipion
7. Roman Walls
8. Agora
9. Saranda Kolones
10. Hellenistic Theatre

1 House of Aion

The god Dionysus features largely in the mosaics in this villa, unearthed in 1983 and dating from the 4th century AD. Other scenes show the god Apollo, the legendary royal beauty Cassiopeia, and the god Aion, after whom the building is named.

2 Villa of Theseus

This villa's mosaics *(above)* are based on a heroic theme: a club-wielding Theseus prepares to take on the Minotaur, watched by Ariadne, while Achilles, champion of the siege of Troy, is shown as an infant.

3 House of Orpheus

Another of the villas *(above)* is still undergoing excavation. A scene of the tragic musician Orpheus pacifying a menagerie of savage beasts is the highlight of the mosaics.

4 House of Dionysus

Named after its mosaics of Dionysus, the god of wine *(below)*, this is the largest of the four opulent villas found at Kato Pafos.

Roman Odeon
The partly restored Roman theatre *(above)*, with its 11 tiers of seats, stands on a hillside overlooking the rest of the site. Built in the early 2nd century AD, it was levelled by an earthquake three centuries later.

Map of Kato Pafos Archaeological Park

Hellenistic Theatre
Overlooking Kato Pafos from the south slope of Fabrica Hill, this semi-circular theatre *(below)* has seven rows of stone benches, cut into the rock of the hillside.

History of Kato Pafos
The kingdom of Pafos is mentioned in passing in Homer's *Iliad,* and the region was settled as early as 1400 BC. Kato Pafos was founded around 320 BC and became the most important city in Cyprus under the Ptolemies of Egypt and then the Roman Empire. The Apostles Paul and Barnabas brought Christianity to the city in AD 45. Pafos remained wealthy and cosmopolitan until it was levelled by earthquakes in AD 365, after which it dwindled into a small fishing settlement. It was revived only with the tourist boom of the 1970s.

Asklipion
The Asklipion was sacred to Asklipios, god of medicine. Its priests were renowned for their healing skills, and it was a hospital as well as a temple of worship.

Agora
The marketplace was the hub of the ancient city's social, political and commercial life and was originally surrounded by a grand colonnade of granite columns.

Roman Walls
Long ramparts and a moat protected Kato Pafos during its heyday as one of the wealthiest cities in Cyprus under the Romans.

Saranda Kolones
This stronghold was erected by the 13th-century Lusignan kings on the remnants of a Byzantine castle. Its massive, battered walls *(left)* and honeycomb of vaults and dungeons are surrounded by a dry moat.

🔟 Akamas Peninsula

The Akamas region is southern Cyprus's last and least developed frontier – a region of spectacular, rugged scenery, sandy coves where turtles nest and dolphins occasionally frolic, clear water, seaside villages and hillsides covered with thick woodland where the last flocks of wild moufflon roam. If empty beaches are what you seek, the Akamas has them, and more: ancient Stone Age dwellings, remnants of Byzantine and Classical settlements and starkly beautiful sea cliffs on the westernmost extremity of the island.

Agios Georgios

⏱ **Visiting Cape Arnaoutis** on a trail bike is popular, but the 36-km (22-mile) round trip is not for novices and can be gruelling in the summer heat. A better bet is to take a boat trip from Latsi, where boats leave for points around the peninsula every morning in summer.

• *Lempa Neolithic Village: Lempa; Map A5; Open 9am–5pm daily; Free*

• *Polis Archaeological Museum: Map A4; 263 22955; Open 8am–2pm Tue–Fri (and 3–6pm Thu except Jul–Aug), 9am–5pm Sat, Sun; Dis. access; Adm €1.70 (Sun free)*

Top 10 Sights

1. Lempa Neolithic Village
2. Coral Bay
3. Agios Georgios & Cape Drepano
4. Lara Bay
5. Cape Arnaoutis
6. Baths of Aphrodite
7. Latsi
8. Polis
9. Drouseia
10. Pano Panagia

Lempa Neolithic Village
Lempa was home to the earliest islanders, who settled here more than 5,500 years ago. Archaeologists have rebuilt dwellings dating from the Chalkolithic era *(above)*.

Coral Bay
No coral, but this sandy beach between two promontories has a tropical air *(above)*. There are sunbeds for hire and a choice of watersports.

Agios Georgios & Cape Drepano
Mosaics of sea creatures adorn the floors of what was once a large Byzantine cathedral, atop the headland of Cape Drepano.

Lara Bay
This sandy crescent *(below)* is one of the south-west's most attractive beaches. It is also a nesting beach for turtles that arrive each year to lay their eggs.

The Lara Turtle Conservation Project battles to save turtle hatchlings and protect Lara Bay from developers

Cape Arnaoutis
This barren but beautiful headland with white limestone cliffs forms the western tip of Cyprus (centre).

Baths of Aphrodite
According to legend, this crystal clear pool is where the goddess bathed with her various paramours. It is said that if you drink from its waters you will fall for the next person you see. Sadly people are not allowed in the pool.

Map of Akamas Peninsula

Drouseia
Worth visiting just for its sweeping views, this picturesque hillside village stands on a wooded ridge high above the beaches of the Akamas peninsula.

Pano Panagia
Amid southern Cyprus's prettiest landscapes is the hill village of Pano Panagia. Nearby is the monastery of Chrysorrogiatissa (above), with a collection of icons.

Latsi
Once a sponge-divers' harbour, Latsi is an attractive little port where fishing boats lie moored to ramshackle wooden jetties (below). There is also a new marina and pleasant beaches of clean pebbles and coarse sand either side of Latsi. Some good fish restaurants by the harbour are worth trying.

Polis
This fast-developing resort(above) still oozes a certain laid-back charm. A small archaeological museum displays relics of the ancient settlement of Arsinoe and Marion, either side of the present-day village, and the small church of Agios Andronikos has some fine frescoes.

Conservation

Environmentalists are fighting a rearguard action to save this last undeveloped stretch of Cyprus coastline from the relentless march of tourism and declare it as Cyprus's only national park. The Akamas is one of the breeding grounds of endangered green and loggerhead turtles, rare breeds of bat, orchids, and many bird species. Ironically, its hinterland has remained unspoiled because for decades it was used as a live firing range by the British Armed Forces.

Sign up for DK's email newsletter on traveldk.com

Left **Lusignan coat of arms** Right **UN patrol on the North–South dividing line**

🔟 Moments in History

Prehistoric Cyprus

1 Neolithic people settled Cyprus more than 10,000 years ago. By 3900 BC copper tools were in use and by 2500 BC Cyprus was part of a Bronze Age civilization with links to Egypt, Asia Minor and the Aegean. In the 12th century BC Achaean Greeks began to oust the original Eteocypriot inhabitants.

Geometric, Archaic and Classical Periods

2 By 1050 BC there were 10 city-states and a flourishing cult of Aphrodite. The wealth of Cyprus lured Phoenicians, who settled at Kition, as well as Assyrian, Egyptian and Persian invaders. In 325 BC Alexander the Great added Cyprus to his empire.

Hellenistic Era

3 After Alexander's death Cyprus fell to the Ptolemy dynasty of Alexandria until 58 BC, when the island was conquered by Rome. The saints Paul and Barnabas converted Sergius Paulus, the Roman governor of Cyprus, to Christianity in AD 45.

Byzantine Era

4 From AD 330 Cyprus was ruled by Constantinople. Earthquakes destroyed coastal cities in the 4th century, but otherwise it was a period of peace. From the mid-7th century the island was devastated by Arab pirates who were not defeated by Emperor Nicephoros Phocas until 965.

Richard the Lionheart

The Lusignans

5 Richard the Lionheart of England seized Cyprus from the Byzantines in 1191 and sold it to the Knights Templar, who in turn sold it to Guy de Lusignan, exiled King of Jerusalem. The Roman Catholic Church supplanted the Greek Orthodox faith.

The Venetians

6 Venice acquired Cyprus in 1489 from the widow of the last Lusignan king, and fortified Nicosia and Famagusta against the Ottomans, but in 1571 the island finally fell to the Turks.

The Ottomans

7 The Turks restored the Orthodox faith whilst encouraging conversion to Islam. Cyprus was seen as a backwater until 1878, when Britain took over in return for supporting Turkey against Russia. In 1914 Britain formally annexed Cyprus.

Independence riots

Independent Cyprus

Cyprus won independence from Britain on 16 August 1960 after a violent national liberation struggle by Greek Cypriots. However, friction between the Greek and Turkish Cypriot communities continued and in 1974 Athens engineered a coup against the Cypriot government with the aim of uniting Cyprus with Greece, while Turkey invaded to protect Turkish Cypriots. Since a ceasefire, the "Green Line", patrolled by UN troops, divides the Turkish-occupied North from the south.

Divided Cyprus

In 1983 the northern part of the island declared itself independent as the Turkish Republic of Northern Cyprus (TRNC). It was, and continues to be, recognized only by Turkey.

EU membership

In April 2003 the Turkish Cypriot authorities decided to allow free movement by Greek Cypriots and visitors to the north of the island. Members of both communities now visit the "other side" on a regular basis. Despite the failure of a UN plan for reunification, Cyprus became a full member of the European Union on 1 May, 2004.

Top 10 Historical Figures

1 Evagoras of Salamis
Evagoras (410–374 BC), king of the city-state of Salamis, conquered much of Cyprus, but was defeated when rival city Amathous allied itself with the Persian Empire.

2 Alexander the Great
Cyprus welcomed Alexander as a liberator from Persian dominance in 325 BC.

3 St Barnabas
St Barnabas, with the Apostle Paul, brought Christianity to Cyprus in 45 AD.

4 Nicephoros Phocas
The Byzantine emperor (963–9) drove the Saracen corsairs from Cyprus.

5 Richard the Lionheart
When the ship carrying Richard's fiancée was driven by storms to Limassol, the English king (1157–99) seized Cyprus (see p19).

6 Guy de Lusignan
Driven from the throne of Jerusalem, Guy (d.1194) bought rulership of Cyprus.

7 Peter I
The Lusignan ruler (1358–69) harried the eastern Mediterranean until assassinated by a cabal of his own nobles.

8 Selim the Sot
The Muslim sultan drove the Venetians from Cyprus after a 10-month siege.

9 Hadjigeorgiakis Kornesios
This intercessor between the feuding Greeks and the Turks became the richest man in Cyprus, until he was beheaded in 1809.

10 Archbishop Makarios
Makarios (1913–77) led the independence campaign and was Cyprus's first president.

Left **Meze dishes** Right **Kolossi Castle**

Aspects of a Multicultural Heritage

1 Art and Architecture

Each of the empires that ruled Cyprus influenced its art and architecture. The Byzantines embraced Orthodox Christianity, which endowed the Troodos churches with their frescoes *(see pp22–3)*; the Lusignans left abbeys and palaces with Gothic elements; and Venetian artists influenced Cypriot icon painters. The decorative Koranic inscriptions which adorn mosques and fountains are an Ottoman legacy, while the British left graceful 19th-century public buildings.

2 Languages and Dialects

In southern Cyprus almost everyone speaks Greek, with only a handful of Turkish speakers. In the North, it's the reverse. Cypriot Greek is a broad dialect that even native Greek speakers from Greece itself sometimes have trouble understanding. Mainland Turks have the same problem with Cypriot Turkish. In both communities, English is a widely spoken, semi-official language – southern road signs are in English and Greek.

3 Religion

Christianity gained an early foothold in Cyprus and most Greek Cypriots are devoutly Orthodox. Turkish Cypriots in the North follow an easy-going form of Islam that doesn't seem to preclude alcohol.

4 Castles

Cyprus is an island of castles. Built to guard harbours and mountain passes, some, such as St Hilarion *(see p105)*, have romantically dramatic backdrops. More grimly purposeful are the fortresses built by the Venetians in the 16th century.

5 Food and Drink

Cyprus owes most of its favourite dishes – from *meze* to *baklava* to *doner kebab* – to the Turks, who also introduced coffee to the island. Other empires contributed to the wine list: Commandaria was first made at Kolossi for the crusader Knights of St John. Red wines were introduced by the Lusignans, while fruity white hock and dry sherry were 19th-century British innovations.

6 Commerce

Cyprus had far-reaching trade ties in ancient and medieval times and the arrival of the Venetians made it part of a commercial empire that spanned the Mediterranean. But it was its proximity to the Suez Canal and the advent of the British that gave it an importance out of all proportion to its size. Today, the island sits at the hub of a trade web that spans western and eastern Europe, the Middle East and the Arabian Gulf.

Orthodox priest

For more about the history of Cyprus **See pp28–9**

Agriculture
From Roman times aqueducts were built to bring water from the mountains to fertile lowland. Grapes were grown from the earliest times; oranges were a Venetian import; cotton and tobacco plantations were Ottoman innovations; and potatoes and tomatoes probably arrived with the British.

Places of Worship
Orthodox places of worship range from tiny stone chapels with Byzantine frescoes to ostentatious modern churches. Mosques, with their domes and minarets, are landmarks in the south as well as the North.

Cypriot musicians

Music
Traditional Cypriot music uses instruments unchanged since Byzantine times, such as the long-necked lute (laouto) and reed pipe (avlos) used by the Greeks and the Turkish short-necked lute (ut), finger-cymbals (kasat) and Turkish oboe (zorna).

Towns
Every Cypriot town has been reincarnated over almost 3,000 years, with new conquerors rebuilding on old foundations. Look for ancient marble and granite column drums and carved capitals built into the walls of medieval castles or supporting the domes of mosques.

Top 10 Prehistoric and Ancient Sites

Amathous
Founded around the 10th century BC, Amathous flourished under the Romans and Byzantines (see pp16–17).

Kourion
This clifftop city is at least 3,300 years old, but the site may have been occupied even earlier (see pp20–21).

Palaia Pafos
Archaeologists have found Chalkolithic idols here from the 4th century BC. ✪ Kouklia • Map B5

Choirokoitia
Stone "beehive huts" (tholoi) and graves show that this settlement was home to as many as 2,000 people as early as 6800 BC (see p71).

Kalavassos
A Neolithic roundhouse, beehive huts and a protective wall have been excavated here (see p74).

Kition
The best preserved ancient Phoenician settlement in Cyprus has a shrine of Astarte, the Asiatic fertility goddess (see p74).

Lempa
This 5,500-year-old Neolithic village has been painstakingly reconstructed by archaeologists (see p85).

Tamassos
This site was known for its copper mines (see p66).

Idalion
Massive walls guard this hillside Bronze Age site, where archaeologists have unearthed statues of Aphrodite (see p66).

Makronissos Tombs
Tombs hollowed into the hillside date from the Neolithic era (see p74).

Left **Larnaka Archaeological Museum** Right **Bowl, Cyprus Museum**

🔟 Galleries and Museums

1 Cyprus Museum, Nicosia
This is the most important museum in Cyprus, with a treasury of archaeological finds and historic relics from the Neolithic era to the heyday of the Byzantine Empire. Among the exhibits are ancient ceramics, superb jewellery and sculptures *(see pp10–11)*.

2 Byzantine Museum and Art Galleries, Nicosia
The magnificent, early Christian Kanakaria mosaics are the gem of this museum, which also has a splendid collection of more than 200 colourful icons mounted in gilt and silver. The oldest date from the 9th century AD.
🔆 *Archbishop Makarios III Foundation, Plateia Archiepiskopou Kyprianou • Map Q2 • Open 9am–4:30pm Mon–Fri, 9am–1pm Sat • Dis. access • Adm*

3 Thalassa Museum, Agia Napa
The newest museum on the island features sea-related artefacts dating from prehistoric times to the late 19th century. A replica of the Kyrenia Ship, the original of which is in Kyrenia Castle, has pride of place. 🔆 *Kryou Nerou 14 • Open Oct–May: 9am–5pm Wed–Sat, 10am–2pm Sun; Jun–Sep: 9am–2pm, 6–10pm Wed–Sun • Dis. access • Adm*

4 Leventis Municipal Museum, Nicosia
An award-winning vernacular history museum is housed in a fine old townhouse, with displays of village and ceremonial costumes, prints, tools and household objects and furniture. There are also several finds here from ancient sites.
🔆 *Ippokratous 17 • Map F3 • Open 10am–4:30pm Tue–Sun • Free*

5 Municipal Arts Centre, Nicosia
An exciting and ever-changing schedule of exhibitions by contemporary Cypriot and international painters is on display here. It is a refreshing change from Classical sculpture and Byzantine icons and frescoes that dominates so much of the island 🔆 *Apostolou Varnava 14 • Map Q2 • Open 10am–3pm, 5–11pm Tue–Sat, 10am–4pm Sun • Dis. access • Free*

6 Pierides Foundation Museum, Larnaka
The oldest private museum on the island, with an eclectic collection of Roman and Byzantine treasures, as well as examples of local island crafts and traditional costumes *(see pp14–15)*.

Lazarus Byzantine Museum

Byzantine Museum & Art Galleries, Nicosia

Lazarus Byzantine Museum, Larnaka

Inside the Church of St Lazarus is an oddly attractive exhibition of 18th- and 19th-century ecclesiastical silver, carved wooden doors and ships' figureheads.
⚅ Plateia Agiou Lazarou • Map M6 • Open Apr–Aug: 8am–12:30pm, 3:30–6:30pm Mon–Fri; Sep–Mar: 8am–12:30pm, 2:30–5pm Mon–Fri • Free

Larnaka Archaeological Museum

Roman glassware, terracotta figurines from ancient sites in the district and painted earthenware, ranging from Neolithic to Roman times, are among the highlights here (see p70).

Larnaka Municipal Art Gallery

Five warehouses have been restored to host exhibitions by Cypriot and foreign artists.
⚅ Plateia Evropis • Map G5 • Open 10am–1pm, 4–6pm Tue–Fri, 10am–1pm Sat–Sun • Dis. access • Free

Cyprus Medieval Museum, Limassol

In the halls of Limassol's castle, this collection features Lusignan swords, Byzantine silver and ceramics, and some fine icons.
⚅ Irinis, Limassol • Map D6 • Open 9am–5pm Mon–Sat, 10am–1pm Sun • Adm

Top 10 Unusual Museums

1 Municipal Museum of Paleontology, Larnaka
Shells and fossils. ⚅ Plateia Evropis • Map G5 • Open 9am–noon Wed–Sun • Free

2 Museum of Cypriot Coinage, Strovolos
Ancient coins. ⚅ Stasinou 51 • Map F3 • Open 8:30am–1:30pm Mon–Fri • Free

3 Cyprus Postal Museum, Nicosia
Philatelic phenomena. ⚅ Agiou Savvas 3B • Map F3 • Open 9am–3pm Mon–Fri • Free

4 Museum of the Liberation Struggle, Nicosia
History of independence. ⚅ Apost. Varnava • Map Q2 • Open 8am–2pm Mon–Fri • Free

5 Shacolas Tower Museum, Nicosia
History of the capital. ⚅ Ledra St • Map P2 • Open 10am–5pm daily (to 8pm Apr–Oct) • Free

6 Cyprus Classic Motorcycle Museum, Nicosia
View over 100 motorcycles. ⚅ Granikou St • Map F3 • Open 9am–1pm, 4–6pm daily • Adm

7 Marine Life Museum, Agia Napa
Stuffed sharks. ⚅ Agias Mavris 25 • Map J4 • Open 9am–2pm Mon–Sat • Adm

8 Lefkara Museum of Traditional Embroidery
Local lace and silverware. ⚅ Map E5 • Open 10am–4pm Mon–Sat • Adm

9 Naive Sculpture Museum, Mazotos
Village life. ⚅ Map F5 • Open 9am–noon daily • Adm

10 National Sea Sponge Exhibition, Limassol
Sponge products. ⚅ Agias Theklas 3 • Map D6 • Open 9am–8pm daily • Free

Left **Limassol Folk Art Museum** Right **Cypriot pottery**

🔟 Folklore Museums

1 Ethnographic Museum of Cyprus, Nicosia

A real treat for anyone with an interest in the hidden histories of Cyprus, this gem of a museum houses textiles, ceramics, wood carvings, copper and brass work, and basket-weaving. ⊗ *Plateia Archiepiskopou Kyprianou • Map Q2 • Open 9am–1:30pm Mon–Fri • Adm*

2 Hadjigeorgiakis Kornesios Ethnological Museum, Nicosia

The double-headed eagle of Byzantium and the lion of Venice are carved above the doorway of this former home of an 18th-century dragoman. The collection includes glass, silver, pottery and furniture from the 18th and 19th centuries *(see p9)*.

3 Fikardou Rural Museum

Vanished village skills live on in two 16th-century houses that have been restored and furnished with period utensils such as an olive press and hand-looms. ⊗ *Houses of Katsinioros and Achilleas Dimitri • Map E4 • Open Jun–Aug: 9:30am–4:30pm Tue–Fri, 9:30am–4pm Sat, 10am–1:30pm Sun; Sep–May: 9am– 4pm Tue–Fri, 9am–3:30pm Sat, 10:30am–2pm Sun • Adm*

4 Limassol Folk Art Museum

Step back in time with more than 500 exhibits here, from fancy costumes worn for holy days to more prosaic farm and house-hold tools *(see p81)*.

5 Fyti Village Weaving Museum

Old wooden handlooms, used by village women until very recently, spinning wheels and other tools of the weaver's trade are displayed here. The resulting colourful wall hangings and blankets are also on show. ⊗ *Map B4 • Open May–Oct: 8am–noon, 2–5pm Mon–Sat; Nov–Apr: 9am–noon, 1–3pm Mon–Sat • Free*

Fyti Village Weaving Museum

6 Fasoula Village Agricultural Museum

Mule and manual labour were supplanted by the pick-up truck and tractor only very recently in Cyprus. This collection of farm tools – some of which hardly changed between pre-Roman times and the 20th century – is an eye-opener. ⊗ *Map D5 • Open 10am–1pm, 2–4pm daily (until 7pm in summer) • Free*

7 Inia Village Folk Art Museum

Basket-weaving was once a universal skill in Cypriot villages but is now a vanishing art. This museum displays the marvels produced by skilled weavers – not only baskets but trays, wall decorations, containers and even fish traps. ◈ *Psathomouseion, Inia • Map A4 • Open Jun–Sep: 11am–1pm, 4–7pm Mon–Fri, 11am–1pm Sat; Oct–May: 11am–1pm, 2–4pm Mon–Fri, 11am–1pm Sat • Free*

Kato Akourdalia Folk Art Museum

A charmingly eccentric collection of heirlooms, old photographs, farm tools, maps and pieces contributed by local people. ◈ *Old School, Kato Akourdalia • Map A4 • Open 8am–2:30pm Mon–Fri (to 5pm Thu) • Adm*

Geroskipou Folk Art Museum, Pafos

The Cypriot love of colour and ornamentation is celebrated in this small museum, with carved and painted gourds, pottery, and embroidered costumes for special occasions. ◈ *Leontiou, Geroskipou • Map A5 • Open 7:30am–2:30pm Mon–Fri (Sep–Jun: to 6pm Thu) • Adm*

Ethnographical Museum, Pafos

The best part of this museum, housed in the prosperous mansion of the influential Eliades family, is the bedroom with its fancy lace, carved furniture and embroidered costumes. The other rooms have interesting displays of pottery and valuable 19th-century antiques *(see p84)*.

Ethnographical Museum, Pafos

Top 10 Arts and Crafts Souvenirs

1 Lace
Delicate hand-made lace from Lefkara and Omodos has been famous for centuries.

2 Rugs and Carpets
Colourful decorative and hard-wearing woollen rugs are made in all sizes, in geometric patterns and stripes of red, orange, yellow and brown.

3 Embroidery
Fine needlework is an age-old Cypriot skill. Embroidered tablecloths, napkins and bed-linen are widely sold.

4 Icons
Genuine antique icons are rare and costly, but many galleries offer beautifully painted copies of museum pieces.

5 Ceramics
Pretty plates, bowls and pitchers in traditional patterns make great gifts, and there are plenty of imaginatively-painted modern pieces too.

6 Gold and Silver
Bracelets, chains, rings and earrings are real bargains. Most gold is 18-carat – look for the hallmark of the Cyprus Goldsmiths Association.

7 Musical Instruments
Antique lutes, cymbals and drums can be found in many antique shops.

8 Reed Baskets
Multicoloured bread baskets are practical and decorative gifts or souvenirs.

9 Kolokitha
These colourful gourds are painted or decorated with carved or pokerwork patterns.

10 Antique Copperware
Look out for old kettles and coffee pots, jugs and antique hubble-bubble pipes in Nicosia.

 For places to buy traditional Cypriot crafts See p91

Left **Panagia tou Sinti Monastery** Right **Agios Georgios Alamanos Convent**

🔟 Monasteries and Convents

Stavrovouni Monastery
With awesome views from its hilltop location, this monastery, founded in the 4th century by St Helena, mother of Emperor Constantine I, is aptly named the "Mountain of the Cross". It is said to house a fragment of the Holy Cross, and its monks, who keep strict vows, are renowned icon painters. No women are allowed to enter *(see p70)*.

Agios Irakleidos Convent
An air of age-old mystery hovers over this oldest of monasteries, founded in AD 400 in honour of Irakleidos. He welcomed St Paul and St Barnabas to Cyprus, who brought with them Christianity, and he thus became the first Bishop of Tamassos. His bones are displayed in an ornate silver reliquary. It is now run by nuns *(see p66)*.

Agios Minas Convent
Graceful white cloisters surround a small 15th-century church and house a community of nuns whose fine icons are sought-after by collectors. ◈ *Map E5 • Open May–Sep: noon–3pm daily; Oct–Mar: noon–2pm daily • Free*

Machairas Monastery
Picturesquely located and sensitively restored, Machairas was founded in 1148. The centuries-old monks' cells, stables and cellars are fascinating, and there is a fine collection of superbly executed icons *(see p66)*.

Agios Georgios Alamanos Convent
Lovingly tended flower and herb gardens surround this small convent, which was founded almost 900 years ago. They are cultivated by a small community of nuns, who also paint attractive icons and make their own honey for sale here. ◈ *Map E6 • Open dawn–dusk daily • Free*

Panagia tis Amasgou
Some wonderful – but unrestored – frescoes dating from the 12th to the 16th centuries are the must-see feature of this nunnery church. It is just one of several important Byzantine churches located in the Kourris Valley, near Limassol. ◈ *Map D5 • Open dawn–dusk daily • Free*

Machairas Monastery

For group-only visits the admission fee is included in cost of escorted tours, which usually include coach transfers too

Kykkos Monastery

This 900-year-old shrine guards a legendary, miracle-working icon of the Virgin Mary. Given to the monastery's founder, the hermit Isaiah, by the Emperor Alexios Comnenos, it has been hidden from profane eyes for

Chrysorrogiatissa Monastery

centuries and remains so to this day. Kykkos is one of the great centres of the Christian Orthodox faith and continues to attract pilgrims from all over the world.
Map C4 • Open Jun–Oct: 10am–6pm daily; Nov–May: 10am–4pm daily • Adm

Chrysorrogiatissa Monastery

The monks of this impressive monastery, devoted to "Our Lady of the Golden Pomegranate" (the symbol of Cyprus), guard a treasury of icons and costly religious ornaments which have been hoarded here since its foundation in the 12th century *(see p85)*. These include an icon of the Virgin Mary, discovered by St Ignatius, and kept on the iconostasis. The monks also make some of Cyprus's finest vintages on the premises, which can be tasted and bought at their winery, Monte Royia *(see p56)*.

Panagia tou Sinti Monastery

Standing alone on the banks of the river Xeros, Panagia tou Sinti is deserted and a little ghostly. Founded in the 16th century, it is one of the island's most important Venetian buildings, and has been awarded the Europa Nostra prize for the sensitive restoration work carried out in the 1990s *(see p85)*.

Agios Neofytos Monastery

The elaborate iron crowns and silken vestments of Orthodox bishops are among the highlights of this monastery's museum. Equally fascinating are the frescoes in its cave-like chapel, a grotto dug by Neofytos, the hermit who founded it in the late 12th century. Map B5 • Open Apr–Oct: 9am–1pm, 2–6pm daily; Nov–Mar: 9am–1pm, 2–4pm daily • Adm

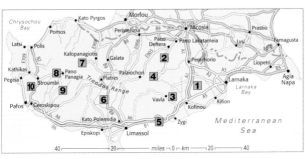

Left **Fyti** Right **Kalavassos**

Scenic Villages

Vavla
With its mellow old stone houses in varying states of disrepair, picturesque Vavla stands among rolling hills with lovely views of the Troodos Mountains. A world away from all the coastal tourist hype. ⊗ *Map E5*

Tochni
Set in a valley amid lush olive groves and vineyards, Tochni is a tranquil village built around a picturesque church. With several sunny tavernas and cafés to choose from, it's a good place to pause for refreshment, particularly after visiting the Neolithic settlement at Choirokoitia or the Agios Minas Monastery, both of which are nearby *(see p74)*.

Kalavassos
This lively village, with great views of the mountains, is centred around a lavishly decorated church. Kalavassos is also an ideal base for exploring the Stone Age tombs at nearby Tenta *(see p31)*, and for walks, cycle rides and horse riding in the surrounding countryside *(see p74)*.

Fikardou
Fikardou *(see p66)* has won a Europa Nostra award for its unique preservation of Cypriot village life and architecture. Some 40 restored houses display traditional red-tiled roofs, mud brick and stone walls, while two 18th-century homes – the Katsinioros and Achilleas Dimitri houses – function as a rural museum *(see p34)*.

Vavla

Kakopetria

The name of this village high in the northern Troodos foothills means "the evil rocks". It was so titled by weary residents who had to clear their fields of hefty stones before they could begin farming. Attractively restored old stone houses and an old-fashioned watermill add to its charm *(see p98).*

Kalopanagiotis

The valley view is the chief charm of this little village, along with a 13th-century frescoed church. In addition, there are some fine old-fashioned mansions, as well as a couple of graceful Venetian bridges spanning fast-running streams. There are good walking trails nearby. ◈ *Map C4*

Fyti

Looking down over slopes and fields to the beaches of the west coast, Fyti is an old-fashioned spot, best known for making lace and woven wall-rugs. *(see p34).* ◈ *Map B4*

Lofou

Sleepy Lofou, set on wooded hilltops in the Troodos foothills, is dazzlingly pretty, with clumps of bougainvillea and morning glory hanging from crumbling buildings. ◈ *Map C5*

Monagri

Silikou

Handy for the picturesque Byzantine churches of the Kourris valley, Silikou is still a working village, not just a tourist spot. Surrounded by olive groves, there is an olive oil museum displaying traditional tools and techniques. ◈ *Map C5*

Monagri

Picturesque Monagri is well worth a visit to see its 12th-century church, Panagia tis Amasgou *(see p36).* The monastery church is unique, with carved stonework dating from the Ottoman era, when it was used as a mosque, and stone pillars salvaged from a Roman temple. Also here is the Monagri Foundation, an art gallery and studio housed in the former Archangelos monastery. The gallery also houses a restored Roman olive press. ◈ *Map D5*

Left **Polis** Right **Protaras**

🔟 Beaches

Agia Napa
Agia Napa's beaches are among the finest in southern Cyprus – and the liveliest, with activities ranging from water-skiiing to bungee jumping and quad-bike riding. Nissi is the closest to town, and gets busy in high summer. Makronissos, longer and less crowded, is 5 km (3 miles) from Agia Napa proper *(see pp12–13)*.

Nissi Beach, Agia Napa

Protaras
"Fig Tree Bay", this resort's favourite beach, has fine white sand and tropical turquoise sea, and is usually a little less hectic than the youth-orientated strands at Agia Napa, only 5 km (3 miles) away. In Protaras itself a range of watersports are available *(see p75)*.

Governor's Beach
A string of small bays of black sand offset by white cliffs, Governor's Beach is a favourite with Cypriots getting away from it all, with plenty of snack-bars and *tavernas*, sunbeds to rent and watersports *(see p88)*.

Evdimou
Despite sea and sand as clean and clear as any on the south coast, Evdimou is uncrowded and undeveloped – but it does have a couple of restaurants catering to hungry sun-worshippers *(see p88)*.

Pissouri
Pissouri is another great beach on Cyprus's southern coast and is popular with families, water-skiers and windsurfers. There are plenty of places to eat and drink along the beach and at Pissouri village inland *(see p88)*.

Pafos
Pafos's best beaches are on the eastern edge of town, near Geroskipou, where the Cyprus Tourism Organization maintains a well-managed, family-friendly strand, and still further east at

Protaras

Pissouri

Floria Beach, next to Pafos airport. Close to the centre of Kato Pafos, there is also a municipal beach beneath shady palm trees, with loungers and umbrellas for hire, a snack bar and restaurant *(see p88).*

Coral Bay
Kolpos ton Koralion, only 8 km (5 miles) north of Pafos, is called Coral Bay by everyone. The sweep of fine sand, covered by rows of sunbeds all summer, is popular with young Cypriots from Larnaka and Limassol. It also hosts live pop concerts on summer evenings *(see p88).*

Lara Bay
Super beaches lie on each side of Cape Lara. South of the cape, there's almost 2 km (1 mile) of uncrowded sand, while to the north there's a shallow bay frequented by loggerhead turtles *(see p26).* The turtle protection group arranges occasional night-time walks

along the beach in egg-laying season, when you can see the turtles struggling ashore. After laying, the eggs are carefully removed to a protected area on the beach where they are safe from dogs, foxes and other predators *(see p89).*

Asprokremos
Those seeking Cyprus's best uncrowded beach need look no further than this super stretch of sand on the north shore of the Akamas Peninsula *(see p89).*

Polis
A long sand-and-pebble beach stretches eastwards along Chrysochou Bay *(see p88),* a 15-minute walk from the centre of Polis – the fastest-growing little resort in western Cyprus. There are less crowded stretches of sand and shingle to the west of the village too. If you're hungry there is a pleasant open-air bar-restaurant and a picnic area beneath eucalyptus trees.

Left **Sailing** Right **Snorkelling area on the Akamas Peninsula**

🔟 Watersports

Swimming

Cyprus's sea is sparklingly clean and crystal clear and ideal for swimming. Most beaches have lifeguards on duty in high season, but look out for red flags, which mean bathing is inadvisable at that time because of high waves or strong currents. Most holiday hotels have at least one large outdoor pool for serious swimmers and a smaller pool for toddlers, but only a few deluxe hotels have indoor pools for use in winter.

Windsurfing

Agia Napa and Protaras have the best windsurfing conditions, but boards can be rented by the hour, half-day or day at all the island's resort hotels and public beaches. The best time of day for windsurfing is often mid- to late afternoon, when a light breeze usually springs up.

Windsurfer

Kiteboarding

This adrenaline-pumping, extreme version of windsurfing involves being towed at high speed by a giant, parachute-like kite. Skilled boarders can make spectacular and daring leaps high into the air before plunging back into the waves. It's just beginning to catch on in Cyprus, and those who dare may find kiteboards for rent at some of Agia Napa's beaches.

Jetskiing

Bouncing from wave to wave on the back of a motorized "waterbike" in imitation of your favourite action hero is a popular beach pastime for locals as well as visitors. Jetskis can be hired at all the resort beaches but, because of the cost of fuel, it's a relatively expensive activity. Lifejackets are compulsory and because of the risk to swimmers it's essential to steer well clear of the lines of coloured buoys which designate swimmer-only stretches of inshore water.

Waterskiing

Limassol, Larnaka and Agia Napa are the best spots for waterskiing, for beginners as well as for experts, because the sea tends to be calmer at these spots. There are dozens of competing water-ski outfits at each resort that will supply all the gear and take you out on the water, so look around for the best price.

Waterskiier

Parascending

You don't need any special skills to strap on a parachute harness and soar into the air as you are pulled along by a fast-moving speedboat, but you do need a certain amount of nerve. The reward is a splendid bird's-eye view of your resort and an exhilarating ride. Again, most resorts have competitive outlets offering this activity.

Snorkelling

There is plenty to see underwater, even within a few yards of the shore if you are a beginner at this sport. The shallows teem with tiny fish, sea anemones and urchins cling to the rocks and, if you are lucky, you may even see an octopus slithering past. But it's well worth heading out to the more rocky shores where there is more to see than on the sandy bottom. One of the best places for snorkelling in Cyprus is the north coast of the Akamas Peninsula (see pp26–7), where rocky coves and tiny islands not too far offshore abound in a variety of sea life, including larger fish such as grouper.

Scuba-diving

Splendid underwater visibility makes Cyprus one of the best diving destinations in the Mediterranean, with some highly rated wreck dives and plenty of professional diving centres. The best diving is off the west coast, and there are dives at all depths and for all levels of expertise. There are PADI and British Sub Aqua Club-approved dive-training centres at all the major resorts (see pp44–5).

Sailing

Skippered yachts can be chartered from island marinas (Larnaka and Limassol are the main centres) by the day or for longer cruises, and smaller dinghies and catamarans are available by the day or half-day from beaches around Agia Napa, Protaras, Limassol and Lakki.

"Banana" Rides

Bright yellow inflatable "bananas" towed at speed by motor boats can carry half a dozen or so passengers. The challenge is to stay aboard while the boat's movement makes the "banana" perform an increasingly extreme series of aquatic maneouvres. Life jackets are essential and most operators insist on an over-15s only policy.

"Banana" ride setting out

Left **St George's Island** Right **Diving in Cyprus**

🔟 Diving and Snorkelling Sites

① Wreck of the Zenobia

This 170-m (555-ft) Swedish truck ferry went down off the coast at Larnaka in 1980 on her maiden voyage (no lives were lost) and lies 43 m (140 ft) underwater. Today it is considered the best dive in the Mediterranean and many claim that it is also one of the best in the world. More than 100 cargo lorries can all be seen, fully intact, and the wreck offers good diving opportunities at all levels. Abundant marine life can be seen around the wreck, including grouper, tuna, conger eels and barracuda. More advanced divers can also descend deeper to explore other interesting parts of the vessel's interior, such as the engine room.

Wreck of the Zenobia

② Wreck of the Vera K

Sunk during World War II, part of this Lebanese freighter's hull lies in only 8 m (26 ft) of water, near the Moulia Rocks just offshore from Geroskipou Beach. It is surrounded by shell casings and amphorae and the wreck attracts plenty of fish. An excellent dive for beginners.

③ St George's Island

Just offshore in 8 m (26 ft) of water off the northwest coast and within the Akamas Marine Reserve, the slopes of this rocky islet abound in marine life, including moray and grouper. You can descend to 35 m (115 ft) to explore the underwater caves. Sheltered from westerly winds, St George's is a good alternative when the west coast sites are not diveable because of high seas or poor visibility.

④ Mismaloya Reef

The Mismaloya Reef abounds in shoals of bass and bream, as well as larger pelagic species. One of the remoter dive sites from Pafos, it takes longer to reach and is more suitable for experienced divers and those who don't mind spending some time at sea.

⑤ Jubilee Shoals

For experienced divers, these shallows, some 35 km (22 miles) offshore in the Pafos area, are a great place to see large pelagics such as tuna and

For details on booking a dive in Cyprus, visit the website www. cydive.com or contact the Cyprus Tourism Organization **See p114**

jack, as well as octopus and moray. The site consists of a vast underwater cliff, with caves, pinnacles and a tunnel and dives offer drop-offs from the 20-m (65-ft) to 60-m (195-ft) levels. Like Mismaloya, this dive site takes longer to get to than most Cyprus dives. An unmissable experience as long as you have the qualifications.

Wreck of the Ektimon
This is an excellent beginner's dive, in only 6 m (19 ft) of water. The *Ektimon* itself, a Greek freighter which ran aground in 1971, has almost disintegrated, but its propellers still mark the spot.

Wreck of the Achilleas
Mystery surrounds the wrecking of the *Achilleas*, which blew up not far from the shore and sank in 1975 in 11 m (36 ft) of water. The wreck is in three sections, at varying depths, and is infested by silvery hordes of smaller sea denizens. Grouper and even a moray or two can also be seen around the ship from time to time.

Amphorae Caves
This is a fascinating offshore cave dive – the clay wine-jar embedded in the roof of one of the caves seems to imply,

School of fish in Cyprus waters

according to archaeologists, that they were once above the waterline and have been drowned over the centuries by seismic movement. Beautiful coral abounds here. Maximum descent is 10 m (30 ft).

Wall Street
This dive involves a plunge into a long, narrow gulley with a profusion of sponges, anemones, soft corals and lots of smaller marine life in depths of 25–30 m (82–98 ft). It is a relatively easy dive, and therefore suitable for beginners, but still offers a spectacular introduction to the underwater world of Cypriot seas.

Petra Gialias
This is a shallow dive set around large offshore boulders. Surrounding these rocks the sea bed attracts huge shoals of smaller fish, as well as the occasional octopus or larger fish such as grouper and barracuda.

Preparing for a dive

Sign up for DK's email newsletter on traveldk.com

Left **Horse riding** Right **Golf course**

🔟 Activities on Land

Golf

Cyprus has perfect golfing weather for much of the year, though some may find July and August uncomfortably hot. Courses on the island, all 18-hole, include the international standard Aphrodite Hills, as well as the Tsada, the Secret Valley and the Elias Country clubs.

⊛ *Aphrodite Hills: between Pafos and Limassol; Map B6; 26 82 82 00; www. aphroditehills.com • Tsada Golf Club: near Pafos; Map B5; 26 64 27 74; www.cyprusgolf.com • Secret Valley Golf Club: 18 km (11 miles) east of Pafos; Map B5; 26 27 40 00, www. cyprusgolf.com • Elias Country Club: www.eliasbeach.com*

Tennis

Tennis fans will find all-weather, floodlit public courts all over Cyprus, and most 5-star hotels and apartment complexes also have floodlit courts.

Karting & Quad-Biking

Would-be Grand Prix winners can test their skills to the limit at karting circuits at Pafos, Polis, Limassol, Larnaka and Agia Napa. Quad-bikes can also be hired at Agia Napa for thrills on the nearby dunes.

Horse Riding

There are equestrian centres and country clubs in Nicosia, Limassol and at Pegeia, near Pafos, all catering to experienced riders as well as offering lessons and equipment for beginners.

Ten-Pin Bowling

The tumbling of skittles can be heard at state-of-the-art air-conditioned bowling centres in Agia Napa (where there is a combined bowling alley and Internet café on the waterfront), Pafos, Larnaka and Limassol. Most are open from noon until 2am.

Angling

Angling is offered year-round from the banks of more than 20 freshwater reservoirs stocked with trout, largemouth bass, carp, pike-perch and roach. Licences are required from the Cyprus Fisheries Department.

⊛ *Cyprus Fisheries Department: Aiolou 13, Nicosia; 22 80 78 62*

Mountain Biking

You don't have to be super-fit to explore Cyprus by mountain bike. Around the resorts there is plenty of fairly flat farmland, and it doesn't take long to find yourself among rolling fields and woodland. With its network of rugged tracks – suitable only for

Mountain biking

mountain bikes or 4WD vehicles – the Akamas Peninsula is ideal territory. Cyprus hosts two annual mountain bike races, the Afxentia International each spring and the Agia Napa International each November.

Mountain Walking
Walking through the cool forests and rugged valleys of the Troodos brings you closer to Cyprus's natural beauty and wildlife than any other way of exploring the island. Spring and autumn are the best times to head for the hills.

Mountain walking

Skiing
There is skiing on 1,950-m (6,400-ft) Mount Olympus from early January to late March, with ski lifts on the north slope of the mountain and at Sun Valley on the south side.

Adrenaline Activities
You don't have to be mad to ascend a shaky, 65-m (210-ft) high tower, then leap from the top attached to a length of elastic cord – but it helps. Agia Napa, that magnet for youthful thrill-seekers, is Cyprus's bungee capital. Also available are the "skycoaster" and the "slingshot" – which instead of sending you plummeting towards the ground, fire you into the air.

Top 10 Cycling Trails

1 Agia Napa Promenade
A mere 9.5 km (6 miles) there and back from central Agia Napa to Agia Thekla, on the flat all the way. ✆ Map J4

2 Around Pafos
Starting by the harbour, take in Pafos's main sights in a 5-km (3-mile) ride. ✆ Map A5

3 Psilodendro Forest
A ride through pine woods from the Troodos Resort to Caledonia Falls – 13 km (8 miles), all downhill. ✆ Map C4

4 Troodos Forest
Starting at Psilo Dendro, a shady 10-km (6-mile) run to Kato Amiantos. ✆ Map C4

5 Troodos to Kryos Potamos
A short but fairly energetic 8 km (5 miles) on wooded slopes. ✆ Map C4

6 Pyrgos to Governor's Beach
A 13-km (8-mile) downhill run from the Troodos foothills ends at one of the island's better beaches. ✆ Map E6

7 Lythrodontas-Lefkara
A challenging 14.5-km (9-mile) ride to the pretty lace-makers' village. ✆ Map E5

8 Akrotiri and the Salt Lake
Look out for flamingoes and pelicans as you make this 30-km (19-mile) circuit (on the flat) of the lagoon. ✆ Map D6

9 Yialias Loop
Mountain breezes take some of the heat out of this 32-km (20-mile) tour, starting and finishing at Lythrodontas. ✆ Map E4

10 The Akamas Peninsula
The 20-km (12.5-mile) journey from Agios Georgios to Latsi is rewarding for tougher riders. ✆ Map A4

The Cyprus Tourism Organization can supply maps for cycling trails See p114

Left **Hiking in Cyprus** Right **Caledonia Trail**

🔟 Walking Trails

Caledonia Trail
This is a fairly gentle amble in the woods, from the Presidential Forest Lodge (where Cypriot presidents come to cool off and think things over) to the famous waterfall in its wooded ravine *(see p98)*. Following the course of the aptly named Kryos Potamos ("Cold River") which never dries up and is perfect for cooling hot feet, look out for birds, butterflies and abundant wild flowers in spring and early summer. Expect to complete the walk in less than two hours at an easy pace. ✪ *Map C5*

Atalanti Trail
A breathtaking panorama rewards walkers on this circular trail, which passes through forests of black pine and centuries-old juniper on its way around the slopes of Mount Olympus, the highest summit of the Troodos massif. Starting and finishing in the square at the centre of the Troodos Resort, the 12-km (7.5-mile) walk takes around five hours. ✪ *Map C4*

Artemis Trail
In spring and autumn, crocuses, cyclamen and anemones greet walkers on this high trail, which starts from the Chionistra-Troodos and Troodos-Prodromos road junction and ends in the centre of Troodos village. Look out for the ruins of a 16th-century fort where a handful of Venetians made a gallant last stand against the Ottoman invaders in 1571. This 8-km (5-mile) walk should take less than three hours. ✪ *Map C4*

Persephone Trail
For those who want to work up an appetite before dinner or burn off calories after lunch, this brisk stroll is ideal. Start just south of Troodos Square in Troodos Resort and walk through lush woods to the Makria Kondarka viewpoint, 1,700 m (5,575 ft) above sea level. The farmlands of the Limassol plain spread out below you. ✪ *Map C4*

Lefkara Circular Trail
Lefkara, with its old stone cottages, is seen at its best from above. This uphill short stroll – only 3 km (2 miles) and about 90 minutes there and back – leads from the village's main street to the hilltop chapel of Metamorfosis tou Sotiros (Transfiguration of the Saviour) and views that sweep over Lefkara and the Agios Minas monastery. ✪ *Map E5*

View of Lefkara

None of the walks is strenuous and they are suitable for people of reasonable fitness, although summer heat can be a problem

Horteri Trail
In the pine-scented heart of Cyprus's largest forest, this is a 5-km (3-mile) uphill hike that is best done in spring or autumn, starting and finishing from the Platanouthkia spring outside Stavros tis Psokas. ✎ Map B4

Selladi tou Stavros
A short stroll through the woods around Stavros covers 3 km (2 miles) and allows visits to the Forest Station with its breeding flock of endangered moufflon sheep. ✎ Map B4

Moufflon

Gerakies Trail
This short walk, starting outside Gerakies, covers 3.5 km (2.5 miles) with fine views of the lush Marathas Valley and the Pafos Forest. ✎ Map C4

Profitis Elias
Starting at Profitis Elias church on the Protaras-Paralimni road, this trail leads through hilly fields and pastures, passing the tiny chapels of Agii Saranta and Agios Ioannis and winding up at Konnos Beach. ✎ Map J4

Agii Anargyri
A stiff clifftop walk, starting at the pretty church of Agii Anargyri above Konnos Beach with a detour to Cape Greco and its lighthouse. ✎ Map J4

Top 10 Animals and Birds

Cyprus Moufflon
Now almost extinct in the wild, this rare native sheep can be seen in sanctuaries.

Flamingo
Greater flamingoes spend the winter on salt lakes near Akrotiri and Larnaka.

Pelican
Although not native to the island, migrating pelicans are sometimes seen resting on Akrotiri's salt lake.

Cyprian Hare
The shy Cyprian hare has been hunted almost to extinction but is sometimes seen by alert walkers.

Cyprus Tree Rat
This nut-eating rodent favours a diet of carob beans and almonds.

Hoopoe
With its zebra-striped crest of quills and pale pink plumage, the hoopoe is graceful and unmistakable.

Rollers and Bee-Eaters
These insect-eating birds, with turquoise, green and yellow plumage, are most often seen in spring.

Cranes
Demoiselle and common cranes fly over Cyprus in spring and autumn, en route between their breeding grounds in Asia Minor and their winter homes in Africa.

Whip Snake
The inoffensive whip snake, glossy black in colour, flees from people but is sometimes seen wriggling at speed across country roads.

Starred Agama
Look for these foot-long mini-dragons scuttling around rocks on the beach or in fields.

Share your travel recommendations on traveldk.com

Left **View from Mount Olympus** Right **Akamas Peninsula**

🔟 Natural Beauty Spots

Akamas Peninsula
A rugged sierra of hills, cloaked in pine forest and fringed by Cyprus's last undeveloped beaches, the Akamas Peninsula is the country's only remaining expanse of wilderness. Turtles lay their eggs on its coasts, and its forest trails – which are best explored with a 4WD vehicle – are a very welcome escape from the bustle of the seaside resorts *(see pp26–7)*.

Petra tou Romiou
Legend claims that Aphrodite, Greek goddess of love and beauty, was born from the sea-foam on this pebbly bay, which is dominated by rugged limestone crags rising from the sea. Other myths say these boulders were hurled at the ships of Saracen corsairs by Digenis Akritas, the paladin of the Byzantine frontier. ◈ *Map B6*

Petra tou Romiou

Caledonia Waterfall
A shady refuge from the summer heat, the 11-m (36-ft) waterfall, plunging into a thickly wooded gully, is named after the swallows *(chelidonia)* which swoop around the falls and pool in summer *(see p98)*.

Cedar Valley
The towering cedars with their spreading green boughs give this valley high in the Tripylos mountain forest its name and aromatic scent. They are the same as the "cedars of Lebanon" mentioned in the Old Testament and prized by the shipbuilders of the ancient world. They grow at altitudes above 900 m (3,000 ft) and are only found here, in the Lebanon, Morocco and the Himalayas. ◈ *Map C4*

Mount Olympus
A jagged and often snow-capped massif, Olympus shares its name with the home of the gods on the Greek mainland. At 1,950 m (6,400 ft), its highest summit, Chionistra, can be seen all over the island *(see p98)*.

Xeros Valley
Graceful arched bridges criss-cross this rugged river bed. Built by the Venetians, they once carried camel-trains bearing copper ore from mountain mines down to Pafos. The Roudias bridge, near Vrecha village, is one of the best preserved. ◈ *Map B5*

Diarizos Valley

Greener and better irrigated than the arid Xeros, the upper Diarizos Valley is studded with medieval churches, farming villages and arched Venetian bridges. The clear-flowing river trickles southwest, and like the Xeros eventually feeds the Asprokremmos reservoir, a mecca for anglers. ❧ *Map C5*

Mount Tripylos

The 1,362-m (4,470-ft) Mount Tripylos, the highest peak in western Cyprus, rises above pine and cedar forests. There are fantastic views over the Tillyrian wilderness to the west and Pafos Forest to the southeast, but it is a little harder to ascend than Mount Olympus. ❧ *Map B4*

Baths of Aphrodite

Cape Arnaoutis & Baths of Aphrodite

The rugged tip of the Akamas Peninsula is a great place to watch the sun plummet into the Mediterranean. Just under 3 km (2 miles) from the cape, a spring, the Baths of Aphrodite, trickles from limestone cliffs into a grotto concealed by fig trees and pink-flowering oleander. ❧ *Map A3*

Salt Lake

This unique wetland is best visited in winter and spring, when its sparkling waters draw flocks of migrant flamingoes and other waterfowl. ❧ *Map D6*

Top 10 Native Flowers

1 Cyclamen
Pink and white Cyprus cyclamen *(Cyclamen cyprium)* flower in woodland in autumn.

2 Anemone
Pink and red anemones or "windflowers" bloom as late as December.

3 Giant Orchid
Growing up to 1 m (3 ft) high, the giant orchid *(barlia robertiana)* is spectacular.

4 Narcissus
White and yellow narcissi, relatives of the daffodil, are brought into bloom by the first autumn showers.

5 Grape Hyacinth
With its bunches of tiny blue globes, the grape hyacinth *(musacri parviflorum)* is another autumn blossom.

6 Cyprus Tulip
Found only in Cyprus, this dark-red tulip *(tulipa cypria)* grows wild in the wastes of the Akamas Peninsula.

7 Lefkara Vetch
Unique to Cyprus, this broad-leafed flower *(astragalus macrocarpus lefkarensis)* is found only in the wooded hills around Lefkara.

8 Cardoon
With its glossy purple crown and spiky leaves, this regal relative of the humble thistle was valued as a food source in hard times.

9 Gladiolus
Great swaths of three-leaved gladioli *(gladiolus triphyllus)* come into vivid flower in early April.

10 Giant Fennel
This towering umbilifer with a greenish-yellow crown provides the aniseed flavouring for *ouzo (see p57)*.

Left **Ascott Pottery jugs** Right **Ostrich Park**

🔟 Children's Attractions

Ocean Aquarium, Protaras

It may be difficult to tear the kids away from this cool cavern full of tanks housing scary piranhas and sharks, menacing morays, stingrays and hundreds of other fascinating denizens of the underwater world. It may be even more difficult to persuade them to go back in the water after they have seen what may lurk beneath. In the aquarium gardens there are also crocodile and turtle ponds and a penguin house. ◈ *Leoforos Protaras • Map J4 • Open 10am–dusk daily • Adm*

Magic Dancing Waters, Protaras

Children (and most likely parents) will be enthralled by this one-hour rainbow-like display of illuminated fountains that seem indeed to make the water dance and change colour to a pro-gramme of classical and pop music themes. Get there early or book in advance from the tourist office, as seats are always at a premium. ◈ *Leoforos Protaras • Map J4 • 9pm daily • Adm*

Ascott Pottery, Protaras

Children can try their hand at turning clay on a potter's wheel at this welcoming commercial pottery. You can also buy their cheerfully coloured plates, bowls, cups and jugs. ◈ *Protaras 200 • Map J4 • Open 8am–sunset Mon–Sat • Free*

Fasouri Watermania, Limassol

Fasouri is the largest and best of the Cyprus water parks, with more than 50 different rides, slides and games, organized activities, thrills such as the near-vertical Kamikaze Ride and gentler paddling for toddlers. There are also two restaurants, three snack bars and a souvenir shop *(see p82)*.

Fasouri Watermania

Pafos Aquarium

An array of colourful fish can be seen in 72 temperature-controlled tanks that have been carefully designed to recreate the natural environment of the species that inhabit them. The aquarium is home to a range of sea- and fresh-water fish, including sea horses, sharks and crocodiles. ⦿ *Kato Pafos • Map A5 • Open 9am–6pm daily • Adm*

Reptile House, Limassol

Kids with a taste for scaly critters and creepy-crawlies will love this collection of snakes, lizards, tortoises (sometimes including newly-hatched babies), scorpions and hairy spiders. Nervous mums and dads may be less enthusiastic. ⦿ *Old Port Roundabout • Map D6 • Open 8am–5pm daily • Adm*

Aphrodite Waterpark, Pafos

Fun for all the family is the theme of this enormous water park, which boasts more than 30 rides and attractions, ranging from fairly gentle slides and floats to exciting five-lane "mat racing", a simulated wave pool, and a shallow pool for toddlers. The park offers a very welcome break from the often oppressive summer heat *(see p85).*

Kikiriko Fun Park, Agia Napa

Kikiriko is Greek for the "cock-a-doodle-do", and one of the main attractions of this park, which is especially designed for children of all ages, is a giant bouncy cockerel. There are also swings, roundabouts, climbing frames and other activities for all the family to enjoy. ⦿ *Leoforos Nissi • Map J4 • Open May–Oct: 4:30pm–midnight daily • Adm*

Aphrodite Waterpark, Pafos

Yellow Submarine, Agia Napa

See the marine world through the portholes of this miniature 30-seat submarine, which cruises the Agia Napa coast and its underwater grottoes. A high point of the two-and-a-half hour cruise is the feeding session, when the skipper attracts dozens of fish to eat food from his fingers. ⦿ *Agia Napa Harbour • Map J4 • Departures 11am and 2:30pm daily • Adm (free for children)*

Ostrich Wonderland, Malounda

Flocks of long-necked ostriches roam in the fields of Europe's largest ostrich ranch. A mini-train carries families around the park to admire the flightless birds in their safari-style enclosures. There's also a restaurant serving ostrich burgers and steaks for lunch, after which you can browse in the on-site shop, where you can buy gigantic ostrich egg ornaments or fresh eggs to cook a family-size omelette. ⦿ *Agios Ioannis Rd • Map E4 • Open daily. May–Oct: 9am–7pm; Nov–Apr: 9am–5pm • Adm*

Left **Meze** Right **Souvlaki**

Cypriot Dishes

Meze
Meze is the keynote of Cypriot cooking – not a single dish, but a massive medley of little samples including delicious dips; tasty prawns, whitebait, squid and other fish; sausages; grilled cheese; and fruit or vegetables that are in season. It's all accompanied by local wine, beer or *ouzo*.

Ofto Kleftiko
This hearty dish is lamb baked in the oven in its own juices until it is so tender that it falls off the bone. Often served with chunky potato chips, it is a good choice for cooler weather.

Ofto kleftiko

Souvla
The simplest and most delicious of Cypriot dishes, *souvla* is made with chunks of pork or lamb, skewered and grilled over charcoal, then served with French fries and a salad of lettuce or cabbage, tomatoes, onions and pickled hot peppers.

Afelia
Lean cubes of tender pork, marinated overnight in red wine and flavoured with cumin, cinnamon, coriander and pepper are the mainstay of this quintessentially Greek Cypriot casserole dish.

Sheftalia
These tasty mini-burgers made with minced pork and aromatic herbs often appear as part of a *meze* array or as an appetizer, but are equally good as a main course, when they are usually served with salad and the inevitable French fries.

Moussaka
Cypriots and Greeks both claim to have invented this filling, oven-cooked casserole. *Moussaka* is often the home-cooked main dish at family occasions such as weddings, christenings and saint's days, and every Cypriot cook has his or her own recipe. The basic ingredients are minced beef or lamb cooked with herbs, red wine and spices between slices of aubergine (eggplant), then covered with a creamy egg and cheese sauce.

Souvlaki
Like *souvla*, only smaller, *souvlaki* is the native fast-food of the island. It's the ideal snack to fend off hunger pangs when exploring on foot. There are simple, friendly grill-cafés in

For what to drink in Cyprus **See p57**

Moussaka

Top 10 Meze Dishes

1 Tahini
Sesame seeds are the key ingredient of this dip, ground with garlic, lemon juice, olive oil and cumin and garnished with flat parsley.

2 Skordalia
This garlic dip is often served as an accompaniment to batter-fried cod and other fish dishes.

3 Karaoli Yahni
Tiny wild snails are a prized Greek Cypriot delicacy. In this dish they are served stewed in tomato sauce.

4 Zalatina
Zalatina, or brawn, is usually served with a relish of capers and a wild spiny pickle called *kapari*.

5 Moungra
Pickled cauliflower is another *meze* favourite to accompany meat snacks, especially in winter.

6 Ochtapodi Krasato
A seafood favourite, chunks of octopus are marinated then simmered in red wine and spiced with cumin and coriander.

7 Barbouni
Tiny red mullet are bony but delicious and served fried.

8 Halloumi Cheese
Grilled halloumi cheese has a chewy texture and is strongly flavoured. It usually accompanies smoked pork, sausages or meat rissoles.

9 Loukanika
Bite-sized smoked sausages are a must with virtually every *meze* meal.

10 Bourekia
If you can find room for dessert, these tiny pastries stuffed with curd cheese and honey will fill the last corner.

every town and village where you can pick up a handful of these skewer-grilled cubes of pork in a pocket of pitta bread, with salad and pickled peppers, to eat on the move.

Louvi me Lahana
This bean salad is a hearty, meat-free option for vegetarians, made with cold black-eye beans mixed with plenty of green vegetables – the exact mix depends on the time of year – olive oil and plenty of freshly squeezed lemon juice.

Koupepia
Cypriots say this dish, made with vine leaves stuffed with minced pork or lamb and rice, is at its best in spring when the young leaves are at their freshest and most tender. In winter, cabbage leaves are sometimes used as a substitute for this reason.

Melintzanes Yiahni
On the Turkish side of the "Green Line", this mélange of aubergines (eggplant) baked in oil with a delicious sauce of garlic and fresh tomatoes is called *imam bayildi*. In either language, it is one of the tastiest vegetarian options that Cyprus has to offer.

Left **Agios Ambrosios** Right **Sterna Winery**

🔟 Wineries and Distilleries

KEO
KEO brews the island's favourite lager beer and a wide range of red, white and sherry-style wines, as well as dessert wines and local versions of international fizzy drinks and mixers. The tour of KEO's modern winery and brewery in Limassol takes about 30 minutes, followed by a tasting session, and is a great way to get to know Cypriot vintages. ◈ *Franklin Roosevelt 1, Limassol • Map D6 • Tours 10am Mon–Fri • Free*

KEO lager sign

Carlsberg
The quirky tour of the Cyprus subsidiary of the huge Danish brewing company includes not only a fascinating glimpse of the brewing and bottling process but admission to a natural history museum and mini-zoo within the brewery grounds. ◈ *Carlsberg Brewery, Latsia • Map F4 • Visits by arrangement • Free*

ETKO
ETKO's best-known product was once its Emva sherry-style wine. However, membership of the European Union has forced the winery (along with its rivals) to rebrand some of its products, as EU rules insist sherry may only come from Spain. A tasting follows the tour. ◈ *Tsiflikoudion 3010, Limassol • Map D6 • Tours 10am daily • Free*

Agios Ambrosios
Ambelida and Anassa (red and white) are the leading labels from this ecological winery, which prides itself on using the minimum of pesticides, fertilizers and additives. ◈ *Archiepiskopou Makariou 25, Agios Ambrosios • Map C5 • 25 94 39 81 • Open by appt • Free*

Sterna Winery
The Pafos region has been famous for wine since antiquity, and a visit to this vineyard is a great way to try some of the best. Among the exhibits is a 200-year-old copper still that continues to be used to produce *zivania*, Cyprus's high-octane moonshine. ◈ *Kathikas village • Map A4 • Open by appt only • Free*

Monte Royia
The monks of Chrysorrogia-tissa monastery (see p85) grow their own grapes on the hillsides around Panagia and produce an excellent, dry white, Agios Andronikos. ◈ *Map B4 • Shop: Open 10am–6pm daily*

Vouni Panagia Winery

Also taking advantage of Panagia's perfect soil and climate is the Vouni Panagia winery, which produces a good dry white called Alina, a hefty red labelled as Plakota and the fine Pampela rosé, all of which can be sampled and bought here. ⓢ *Vouni • Map C5 • Open 8am–5pm daily • Free*

Tsiakkas vineyards

Tsiakkas Winery

Set high in the Troodos Mountains, Tsiakkas has won awards for its red, white and rosé wines, made by blending traditional grape varieties with foreign imports. ⓢ *Pitsylias, near Pelendri • Map D5 • Open 9am–5pm daily • Free*

Marki Winery

Look out for the reliable and well-priced "Kilani Village" red and white wines from this village winery. ⓢ *Agia Mavri, Kilani • Map C5 • 25 47 02 61 • Open by appt • Free*

Fikardos

One of the best of the Pafos winemakers, making red and white wines in a variety of styles. ⓢ *Mesogi Industrial Estate • Map B5 • 26 94 98 14 • Open 8am–4pm Mon–Fri; 8am–1pm Sat • Free*

Top 10 Drinks

Ouzo
Sweet and aniseed flavoured, *ouzo* turns a milky white when water is added. An acquired taste.

Zivania
Brace yourself for this fiery, *grappa*-style spirit. Not to be consumed in quantity.

Brandy
Drunk on its own or in a variety of cocktails. The brandy sour is the island's own cocktail and very palatable.

Wine
Red and white wines from Cyprus are generally unpretentious, quaffable and cheap, and quality continues to improve.

Filfar
This sticky-sweet liqueur, distilled from Cyprus oranges, is best enjoyed with coffee.

Mosphilo
Unique to Cyprus, *mosphilo* is a sweet-sour liqueur distilled from the red berries of the hawthorn tree.

Beers
Brewed in Cyprus are KEO, Carlsberg and Five Beer, plus Leon – first produced in 1937 and recently reintroduced. Most foreign beers are also available everywhere.

Coffee
Starbucks and Costa Coffee are here, but you should also try *ellinikos kafes*, served in a tiny cup and thick with sugar and caffeine.

Cocktails
From the brandy sour to the saucy Sex on the Beach, Cypriot bars offer an extensive cocktail list.

Soft Drinks
All the big-brand soft drinks, plus convincing local imitations, are available.

Left **Carnival, Limassol** Right **Anthistiria**

🔟 Cultural and Traditional Festivals

1 Carnival, Limassol
Limassol comes to life during the 10 days before Lent, when islanders indulge themselves with feasts and fancy-dress parades. Carnival is also celebrated elsewhere on the island, but Limassol's celebrations are traditionally the liveliest and most entertaining. ◐ *Feb–Mar*

2 Anthistiria, Larnaka and Pafos
Cyprus blossoms under the spring sun and in May the streets of Larnaka and Pafos are draped in blooms during flower festivals. They climax with parades of floats drowned in colourful garlands. ◐ *May*

3 Shakespeare Festival, Kourion
Kourion's amphitheatre with its magnificent hillside location *(see pp20–21)* makes the perfect venue for this summer festival of drama. Kourion is also used regularly for concerts, often

Dance performance, Kourion

featuring internationally-known Greek artists, such as Nana Mouskouri, Vicky Leandros and Demis Roussos. ◐ *Jun–Jul*

4 Larnaka International Festival of Music, Theatre and Dance
Larnaka takes its place in the limelight when musicians, dancers and actors – many of them from Greece, Balkan and eastern European countries and the former Soviet Union – make the pilgrimage to what has become one of the island's leading cultural events. ◐ *Jul*

5 Mountain Villages Cultural Week, Limassol District
Dancers and musicians revive the all-but-vanished traditions of Cyprus's villages during this event, which aims to keep the spark of the island's culture alive. The week offers a glimpse of village life as it was before tourism, television and mobile phones came to places such as Kilani, Omodos, Pera Pedi, Troodos and Mandria ◐ *Jul*

6 Kourris Valley Commandaria Festival
Wine flows freely and there is dancing in the streets as the mountainous Kourris Valley's vineyard villages – Alassa, Agios Georgios, Doros, Lania, Monagri and Silikou – celebrate the start of the grape harvest. Visitors are welcome to join in, eat, drink and be merry. ◐ *Aug*

 Details of venues and dates, updated monthly by the Cyprus Tourism Organization, can be found at www.visitcyprus.org

International Festival of Ancient Greek Drama, Pafos

The works of ancient playwrights such as Sophocles, Euripides and Aristophanes leap back to life in Pafos's ancient odeon during this internationally renowned cultural event. It attracts performers and directors from Cyprus, Greece and further afield. ◈ Aug

Limassol Wine Festival

This is the perfect time to sample Cyprus's dozens of wines in depth, at length and, best of all, for free. Limassol's wine-makers celebrate by sponsoring 10 days of wine tastings, held in the city's attractive municipal gardens. The whole event is accompanied with outdoor live music and dancing in the evenings. ◈ Sep

Pafos Aphrodite Opera Festival

A month after the Greek drama festival, the area in front of Pafos castle comes alive again as the setting for three days of opera, performed by an esteemed international cast. This popular autumn event is one of the highlights of the country's cultural calendar. ◈ Sep

Agia Napa International Festival

Agia Napa's lively annual festival has become a magnet for many folk dancers and traditional musicians, especially those from other Mediterranean countries and from Eastern Europe. The event also brings theatre groups, opera companies and international singers to the resort for a particularly dazzling weekend of performances in the island's busiest esort. ◈ Sep

Top 10 Orthodox Religious Festivals

Agios Vassilios
On St Basil's Day islanders have a meal which culminates with vasilopitta, a sweet loaf containing a coin that brings good luck to its finder. ◈ 1 Jan

Fota (Epiphany)
In harbour towns youths vie for the honour of retrieving a crucifix thrown into the sea. ◈ 6 Jan

Green Monday, Limassol
After the Carnival festivities, islanders feast on flatulence-inducing beans and pulses with the aim of purging the devil from their bodies. ◈ Feb

Annunciation
Annunciation is a Greek national holiday. ◈ 25 Mar

Good Friday
Christ's effigy, decorated with flowers, is carried solemnly through the streets at nightfall. ◈ Mar, Apr or May

Easter Saturday
After midnight mass, villagers take home a taper lit from a blessed candle. ◈ Mar, Apr or May

Easter Sunday
Villagers roast a goat; town-dwellers head to grill restaurants. ◈ Mar, Apr or May

Kataklysmos
Noah's escape from the Flood is celebrated with processions and music. ◈ May or Jun

Assumption
Assumption is marked by pilgrimages to the island's many churches bearing the name of the Virgin. ◈ 15 Aug

Christmas
Christmas is celebrated by islanders as well as holiday-makers. ◈ 25 Dec

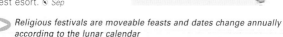

Religious festivals are moveable feasts and dates change annually according to the lunar calendar

AROUND CYPRUS

CYPRUS'S TOP 10

Left **Strovolos** Right **Archbishop's Palace, Nicosia**

Central Cyprus

STEEPED IN HIDDEN HISTORIES, *the heartland of Cyprus is full of variety, from the bustle of Nicosia, the island's capital, to old-fashioned villages and age-old churches in the foothills of the Troodos mountain range. This is a part of Cyprus that remains surprisingly unexplored by many visitors, yet it repays investigation. It is the best place to see the true face of the island – Nicosia is far less absorbed in tourism than the coastal resorts and the same is true of the outlying villages. The walled city has an atmosphere all of its own, with sleepy, sunbaked streets and authentic cafés, and the opportunity to experience the reality of the divided city first-hand by crossing over to the Turkish-occupied North for a day.*

🔟 Sights

1. Nicosia Walled City
2. Cyprus Museum
3. Aglandjia
4. Strovolos
5. Agios Dometios
6. Kaimakli
7. Latsia
8. Lythrodontas
9. Dali
10. Potamia

Laiki Geitonia, Nicosia

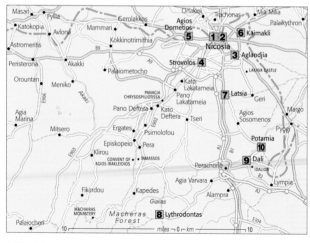

Nicosia

Nicosia Walled City

Cyprus's capital city is a mélange of medieval, colonial and modern influences. Within the brooding ramparts built by the Venetians are the narrow pedestrian streets and prettily restored buildings of the Laiki Geitonia pedestrianized district, full of souvenir shops and cafés. But the city also offers more than a day's worth of museums and heritage sites celebrating every aspect of the Nicosia's history, from its ancient past to its traditional crafts (see pp8–9).

Cyprus Museum

A treasury of archaeological finds here, uncovered from sites all over Cyprus, wonderfully illustrate the island's historic past and make this the most fascinating of all its many museums. Exhibits highlight the marvellous skills of sculptors, metalworkers, potters, painters and other craftsmen across more than four millennia (see pp10–11).

Aglandjia

Not so long ago, Aglandjia, which dates back as far as 3888 BC, was a village community in its own right, thriving on agriculture, stockbreeding and quarrying. Today, although it has become virtually a suburb of Nicosia, it still retains a village ambience, with a handful of pretty 18th-century churches. Among these is the one-domed, arch-roofed Agiou Georgiou church, which contains a woodcut iconostasis decorated with images of baskets and flowers. ◉ Map F3

Strovolos

The unique Pancyprian Geographical Museum – the only one of its kind in Cyprus – within an attractively restored traditional building is the main reason for visiting Strovolos. It is dedicated to the island's geology, with displays of minerals, especially copper, which made Cyprus wealthy in pre-Christian times, and semiprecious stones. The town itself is built around the 18th-century church of Agios Georgios (one of half a dozen churches named after St George in this part of Cyprus). Like Aglandjia, Strovolos is now on the verge of becoming a suburb of Nicosia. ◉ Map F3 • Pancyprian Geographical Museum: Leoforos Strovolou 100; Open 8am–2:30pm Mon–Fri (also 3–6pm Thu) • Adm

Agios Dometios

Agios Dometios
The pretty, late 17th-century church of Agios Dometios is the main attraction of this village community, quite unchanged by time. Although it's on the outskirts of the capital, Agios Dometios still moves at its own leisurely pace, and it's a nice spot to stop for a coffee or a cold drink. ◈ *Map E3*

Kaimakli
Two pretty churches are the jewels of this village. Although they are not that old by Cypriot standards – the Church of the Archangel dates from the 18th-century and the church of Agia Barbara is a mere late 19th-century addition – they are worth visiting nonetheless for the excess of ornate carving, silver-framed icons and votive candles that are so typical of the Orthodox faith. ◈ *Map F3 • Open daily • Dis. access • Free*

Latsia
Plunging through rugged scenery, the Kakaristra Gorge at Latsia is this hillside village's most important landmark. It can be explored alone, or with a local guide. Incongruously but entertainingly, the nearby Carlsberg

Brewery *(see p56)*, just outside the village, is open for visits and houses the Photos Photiades Foundation's natural history museum, an exotic glory-hole of stuffed, fossilized and pickled snakes, birds, mammals and marine creatures. ◈ *Map F4*
• *Cyprus Museum of Natural History, Carlsberg Brewery: Open 9am–4:30pm Mon–Fri; Dis. access; Free*

Lythrodontas
Located some 25 km (15 miles) south of Nicosia, this village is best known for its olive groves (Lythrodontas claims to have more olive trees than any other village in Cyprus) and "Avli", a beautifully restored complex of traditional buildings offering accommodation. The nearby abandoned Monastery of Prophitis Elias is also worth a visit. ◈ *Map E4*

Dali
A lively farming village that comprises not much more than a main street lined with shops and a scattering of traditional cafés and a village church, Dali offers a taste of Cypriot life largely untainted by tourism. It takes its name from one of Cyprus's most ancient city states, Idalion, which archaeologists are continuing to explore nearby. Also nearby are the much ruined, but still

Dali

The Green Line

The Green Line divides both Cyprus and the city of Nicosia in two and marks the southern extent of the Turkish army's advance in 1974. Stretches of barbed wire, metal fence and sandbags and a no-man's-land of derelict homes and deserted shops separate the two halves of the city. Foreign visitors and Greek Cypriots in Nicosia may visit the north on foot via the Ledra Palace crossing point or by car via the Agios Dometios crossing point. In the Larnaka and Famagusta districts, there are crossing points for cars at Pergamos and Strovilia respectively. If taking a car to the north, you need to take out insurance at the crossing point: CY£10 for three days.

haunting, remains of a Gothic church and summer palace of the Lusignan kings, who came here to escape the heat of summer on the coasts (see p66). ◎ Map F4

Potamia

If you want to see the effects of the division of the island since 1974 on a rural community, Potamia is a good place to start. Until 1974, it was approximately half Greek and half Turkish Cypriot, but today only a handful of Turkish Cypriots remain, while exiled Greek Cypriots have moved into properties abandoned by those who left. The village overlooks the "buffer zone" that divides the south of the island from the occupied North. Potamia was also the site of a fortified royal villa, built in the 14th century for the Lusignan King James I but destroyed by Ottoman invaders 1426. A ruined shell on the outskirts of the modern village is all that now remains. ◎ Map F4

A Morning Shopping in Nicosia

Start your day at the top of Stasicratous and window-shop your way south past ranks of designer stores, then double back along busy Archiepiskopou Makariou III, stopping for a cold drink at one of the street's hip cafés.

Cross Plateia Eleftherias and enter **Laiki Geitonia** (see p8). This area has been restored as a sanitized version of an old-fashioned Nicosia neigh-bourhood. You'll find souvenirs aplenty here – some authentic, some amusing and some trashy. The Diakroniki Gallery at Aristokyprou 2B is a good place to seek out original and facsimile prints and engravings. Nearby, at Ippokratous 2, you can find copies of Byzantine silverware at the Leventis Museum Gift shop.

Nicosia's main shopping street, Odos Lidras (Ledra Street), runs north from Laiki Geitonia. It too is pedestrianized, but it could hardly be more different with its big-name department stores and smaller shops doing a thriving trade in copies of designer sunglasses.

At Plateia Faneromenis, turn right and wander across the square to the Central Market, off Plateia Palaiou Dimarchiou, for a look at how the locals shop: fruit and vegetables, fresh olives, feta cheese and dried herbs are sold from dozens of stalls in this venerable emporium.

If all this food has made you hungry, enjoy a fish lunch at **Kalymnos Fish Tavern** (see p67).

Around Cyprus – Central Cyprus

Left **Fikardou** Right **Machairas Monastery**

💯 Villages and Churches

Machairas Monastery
This monastery was founded in 1148 by two hermits guided by divine intervention to an icon of the Virgin, painted by Luke the Evangelist. The icon survived fires which damaged the monastery in 1530 and 1892 – proof, to believers, of its miraculous powers *(see p36)*. 🚩 *Map E4*

Fikardou
The hill village of Fikardou has won tourism awards for its living museum that shows Cyprus village life as it was until just a few decades ago *(see p34)*. 🚩 *Map E4*

Agios Irakleidios Convent
One of the oldest Christian communities in Cyprus, the chapel here dates from the 15th century. It lay in ruins before being restored in the 1960s. 🚩 *Map E4* • Open 8:30am–5:30pm daily • Free

Tamassos
Tamassos was one of the earliest cities on the island (6th century BC) and grew wealthy from its copper mines, which were famed throughout the ancient world. 🚩 *Map E4* • Open 9:30am–3.30pm daily • Adm

Pera Chorio
Saints, martyrs, emperors and demons are depicted in wall-paintings within the Byzantine church of Agioi Apostoloi in this small village near Dali. 🚩 *Map F4*

Ancient Idalion
Dali is a farming village that takes its name from the ancient city-state of Idalion. Aphrodite's lover, Adonis, was killed by the boar of Idalion and the red flowers that bloom here are deemed tokens of his death. 🚩 *Map F4*

Agios Sozomenos
In the deserted village of Agios Sozomenos is the medieval church of Agios Mamas, with Gothic arches. 🚩 *Map F4*

Panagia Chrysospiliotissa Church
Catacombs dug into the hillside show that this church dates from early Christian times, when believers worshipped in secret for fear of persecution. 🚩 *Deftera* • Map E4 • Open dawn-dusk daily • Free

La Cava Castle
Toppled ramparts mark the site of this Crusader keep. 🚩 *Map F3* • Closed to the public

Peristerona
A 10th-century church with wall paintings dates from the 12th and 15th centuries. 🚩 *Map D3*

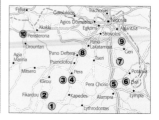

Price Categories

For a three-course meal for one with half a bottle of wine (or equivalent meal), taxes and extra charges.		
€	€10–€15	
€€	€15–€25	
€€€	€25–€35	
€€€€	€35–€50	
€€€€€	over €50	

Above **Kalymnos Fish Tavern**

🔟 Nicosia Cafés and Restaurants

Kalymnos Fish Tavern
Unquestionably the best fish restaurant in Nicosia, Kalymnos attracts the city's movers and shakers. Superb seafood and a good wine list. Reservations recommended. ❧ *Zena Gunther St 11 • Map P3 • 226 72423 • €€€€€*

Abu Faysal
This attractive Lebanese restaurant, decorated with tapestries and wood floors, serves wonderful grilled meat and fish accompanied by spicy sauces. ❧ *Klimentos 31 • Map Q3 • 227 60353 • Closed Mon • €*

Aegeo Tavern
Set in an old house, this traditional taverna serves excellent *meze*. In summer, dining is available in the pleasant courtyard or on the balcony if you book ahead. ❧ *Ektoros 40 • Map Q3 • 224 33297 • €€*

Irinias
The Greek Cypriot food at Irinias is a long-standing favourite – make a reservation (or go early in the evening) to be sure of getting a table. ❧ *Arch. Kyprianos 64A, Strovolos • Map F3 • 224 22860 • €€*

Da Capo
To see and be seen, look no further than Da Capo, where the clientele dress mainly in black and where sunglasses are mandatory day and night. Good coffee and pastries. ❧ *Makarios 30B • Map P3 • 227 57427 • Dis. access • €€€*

Le Café
Young, designer-clad Nicosians favour this colourful café. The noise of full-volume conversation – face to face or by mobile phone, sometimes simultaneously – drowns out the traffic. ❧ *Makarios 16 • Map P3 • 227 55151 • Dis. access • €€€€*

Pralina
Nicosia's "ladies who lunch" favour Pralina, on the city's smartest shopping street, for coffee and pastries. Those who turn up in shorts will feel conspicuously under-dressed. ❧ *Stasikratous 31 • Map P3 • 226 60491 • Dis. access • €€€€*

Kavouri Fish Tavern
On the outskirts of town, Kavouri has a well-earned reputation with a loyal local following for its lavish seafood *meze*. ❧ *Strovolos 125, Strovolos • Map F3 • 224 25153 • €€€*

Trattoria Romantica,
A cut above the run of Italian restaurants, this stylish place with tables on a patio serves well-made pasta dishes and other favourites. ❧ *Eva Palikarides 13 • Map P3 • 223 76161 • €€€€*

Bagatelle
Elegant French restaurant serving classic Gallic cuisine such as frogs' legs and duck *à l'orange*. Live piano music at night. ❧ *Kyriakos Matsis 16 • Map P3 • 223 17870 • Closed Sun • €€€€*

Note: *Unless otherwise stated, all restaurants accept credit cards and serve vegetarian meals*

Left **Chapelle Royale fresco** Right **Lefkara**

Southeast Cyprus

LEGENDARY NIGHTLIFE AND EQUALLY LEGENDARY BEACHES *are what draw most of the hundreds of thousands of visitors who come to Cyprus's southern and eastern shores each summer. Many of them get no further than the sun-loungers, hotel pools, clubs and bars of Agia Napa or Protaras – both former fishing villages that have rocketed to holiday resort prominence in a relatively small number of years. Larnaka, a busy commercial port as well as Cyprus's business hub, also has an excellent beach that draws the crowds. Yet there is much more to see in this fascinating region. Among fields and olive groves in the gently rolling hills that give way to the mountains of central Cyprus are tiny Byzantine churches, many of which shelter age-old icons and frescoes. Remarkable Stone Age settlements give off an aura of lost histories. And, tucked away in hidden valleys, are old-fashioned villages where you can shop for traditional handicrafts or sip a cup of Cypriot coffee in a pavement café and simply watch the slow pace of life go by.*

TOP 10 Sights

1 Agia Napa
2 Protaras
3 Waterworld
4 Pieries Foundation Museum, Larnaka
5 Larnaka Fort and District Medieval Museum
6 Larnaka Archaeological Museum
7 Stavrovouni Monastery
8 Chapelle Royale
9 Lefkara
10 Choirokoitia Neolithic Settlement

Stavrovouni Monastery

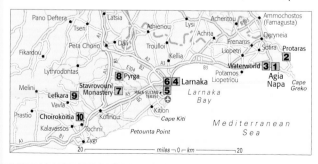

Share your travel recommendations on traveldk.com

Agia Napa harbour

Agia Napa

Agia Napa, on the south shore of a peninsula that juts towards Cyprus's southeast tip, has risen to fame as one of the world's great dance party destinations, but there is much more than mere nightlife to this purpose-built sunshine resort. Agia Napa's core – and the favourite evening rendezvous for party-goers – is its main square, which is packed with bars and café tables. Yet, only steps away from the hedonistic crowds is a tranquil oasis, the medieval Agia Napa Monastery, while down on the sea front the Limnaki ("little harbour") still has some of its village character, even if, these days, the fishing boats are out-numbered by excursion vessels carrying holidaymakers to outlying beaches (see pp12–13).

Protaras

On the east coast of Cyprus and only 8 km (5 miles) from Agia Napa, Protaras has mushroomed into prominence around a clutch of sandy beaches where the warm, shallow water is a vivid turquoise. During the day, the

Agia Napa's Club Scene

Agia Napa was discovered by British clubbers in the late 1990s and quickly soared to prominence as Europe's top summer nightlife destination, rivalling even Ibiza for a couple of years. Up to a dozen top clubs pulse with sounds from big-name DJs all summer. Things start late – most clubs don't open until around 1am and stay open until around 4pm – but there is a lively pre-club scene in the bars around Agia Napa Square.

beaches are lined with sunbathers while the sea is dotted with the bright sails of windsurfers and catamarans. At night, Protaras comes into its cosmopolitan own, with a main street lined with bars, cafés and restaurants to suit all tastes. There are plenty of excursions to be made to nearby sights and attractions, such as Fig Tree Bay (see p75). Map J4

Waterworld

The flumes and lagoons of Waterworld are an Agia Napa landmark, 2 km (1 mile) west of the town centre. There's plenty of family fun here, with gentle rides and shallow pools for younger kids and roller-coasters and slides for teenagers. Agia Thekla 13, Agia Napa • Map J4 • Open Apr–Nov: 10am–6pm daily • Adm

Protaras

Pierides Foundation Museum, Larnaka

The Pierides Museum was founded by a wealthy collector and philanthropist, and displays as its most colourful and interesting exhibits village costumes and old-fashioned tools and farm implements, some of which, astonishingly, only ceased to be in everyday use as recently as a decade ago. There's also a huge collection of delicate Roman glass and some fine old embroidery, lace and silver jewellery. In addition, this well laid-out collection features some fascinating ancient relics, most notably the famous "Howling Man", a 5,000-year-old terracotta figure. Red-and-black bowls and vases and terracotta figures excavated from archaeological sites all over Cyprus have found a home here, as well as a collection of medieval maps, weapons and armour. The Pierides Foundation also sponsors Larnaca's fossil museum *(see pp14–15)*.

Larnaka Fort and District Medieval Museum

Huge rusting cannons stand guard over the waterfront from the battlements of Larnaka's medieval fort, from which there are good views of the bay. Inside, the District Medieval Museum's collection occupies a gallery on the first floor, with ferocious swords and daggers, medieval armour and flintlock muskets outshining an assortment of 12th- to 18th-century pottery and displays of Byzantine, Lusignan and Ottoman odds and ends. Occasionally in summer open-air theatrical performances are staged here ✪ *Finikoudes Beach, Larnaka • Map M6 • Open Jan, Feb, Nov & Dec: 9am–5pm Mon–Fri (to 6:30pm Mar, Apr, Sep & Oct; to 7:30pm Jul & Aug) • Adm*

Cannon, Larnaka Fort

Larnaka Archaeological Museum

Carved limestone column drums and capitals from ancient sites stand in the garden of the Archaeological Museum. Inside is one of the best introductions to the southeast's fascinating archaeological sites, with its displays of Stone Age, Bronze Age and Roman discoveries brought here from Choirokoitia, Kalavassos and many other local excavations *(see p32)*. ✪ *Kalogreon Square • Map L4 • Open 9am–2:30pm Mon–Fri (and 3–5pm Thu Sep–Jun) • Adm*

Stavrovouni Monastery

This impressive monastic eyrie, founded by a Byzantine empress (the mother of Constantine the Great) is poised high above the coastal plains on a 700-m (2,300-ft) crag in the foothills of the Troodos mountain range. Still home to a community of 20 monks, it claims as its most holy relic a fragment of the True Cross – its name in Greek means "Mountain of the Cross" *(see p36)*. ✪ *Map F5 • Open Sep–Mar: 8am–noon, 2–5pm daily; Apr–Aug: 8am–noon, 3–6pm daily • Free*

Chapelle Royale
This village chapel, dedicated to St Catherine, was built by King Janus and his queen, Charlotte de Bourbon, in 1421. Within are colourful remnants of some unique frescoes. ⊗ *Pyrga • Map F5 • Open daily on request • Adm*

Lefkara
Famed for the lace-making skills of its womenfolk and the silversmithing skills of its men, Lefkara is home to a multitude of craft shops selling lace, embroidery and jewellery. If you're not in the mood to buy, marvel instead at the beautifully made treasures in the Museum of Traditional Embroidery and Silversmithing. ⊗ *Map E5 • Museum: Open 9:30am–4pm Mon–Thu, 10am–4pm Fri & Sat • Adm*

Choirokoitia Neolithic Settlement
An aura of almost unimaginable age hangs over Choirokoitia, where archaeologists have discovered the foundations of a settlement that thrived on this hilltop almost 9,000 years ago. Some of the round stone houses have been reconstructed, and UNESCO has declared it a World Heritage Site. ⊗ *Map E5 • Open 9am–5pm daily (May–Aug: 9am–7:30pm Mon–Fri, 9am–5pm Sat & Sun) • Adm*

Choirokoitia Neolithic Settlement

A Half-Day Walk from Agia Napa to Protaras

This 12-km (7.5-mile) walk, taking about three or four hours (allowing time for swimming stops) is an ideal way to burn off a night's excesses. But for the less energetic, Agia Napa has plenty of bicycle rental shops and an asphalted bike trail leads round the headland that separates the two resorts. Take plenty of water and wear high-factor sunblock, especially between June and September.

Starting the walk at Agia Napa's harbour, head east along the coast, past Limnaki and **Kryo Nero** beaches *(see p75)*. As you leave the last of Agia Napa's resort hotels behind, the coast becomes progressively rockier, towards the rugged headland of **Cape Gkreko** *(see p13)* and its landmark radar masts. Kermia beach, 4 km (2.5 miles) east of Agia Napa, is a good place to stop for a dip before setting off across country.

The route now skirts the misleadingly named Agia Napa Forest, which is actually an area of native juniper scrub, then passes the scant remnants of a temple to Aphrodite before plunging down to the blue water and pebbles of tiny **Konnos Bay** *(see p75)*, overlooked by the little white church of Anargyroi.

From here, you can head gradually back into resort territory before reaching **Protaras** *(see p69)* for a well-earned cold drink. If you're on foot, there are plenty of taxis to take you back to Agia Napa.

Following pages: **Stavrovouni Monastery**

Left **Hala Sultan Tekke** Right **Kition**

Best of the Rest

1 Kition
Foundations of Mycenaean temples dating from the 13th century BC hint at a lost city beneath Larnaca's streets. There are remnants of ancient temples, sacrificial altars and a copper-smith's workshop. ◈ *Archiepiskopou Kyprianou, Chrysopolitissa, Larnaka • Map G5 • Open 9am–2:30pm Mon–Wed & Fri; 9am–5pm Thu • Adm*

2 Hala Sultan Tekke
Hala Sultan Tekke is prettiest in winter and spring when its domes and spires are reflected in the waters of Larnaka's Salt Lake. Within the mosque is the tomb of Umm Haram, aunt of the prophet Mohammed. ◈ *Dromolaxia • Map G5 • Open daily. Nov–Mar: 9am–5pm (to 6pm Apr, May, Sep & Oct); Jun–Aug: 7:30am–7:30pm • Dis. access • Adm*

3 Tochni
Surrounded by vineyards and farmland, Tochni has a traditional feel, with old stone houses lining narrow streets. ◈ *Map E5*

4 Kalavassos
This village nestles beside a stream in a huddle of old stone houses. Nearby, in the Neolithic village of Tenta, Stone Age skeletons have been found. ◈ *Map E5*

5 Makronissos Tombs
Cut into the limestone rock are 20 chamber tombs, dating from the Neolithic era but also used by the Romans and Byzantines. ◈ *Map J4 • Open daily • Free*

6 Deryneia
This farming village looks over to the Turkish-occupied North, towards Famagusta, and you can make out the battlements of the walled city in the distance. Deryneia also has three pretty churches: 15th-century Agia Marina, 17th-century Agios Georgios and the church of the Panagia *(see p13)*. ◈ *Map J4*

7 Sotira
Sotira is home to five Byzantine churches, the most important of which is Metamorphosis tou Sotiros, from which the village takes its name. ◈ *Map J4*

8 Liopetri
Woven baskets dangling outside shops are an indication that the craft for which this village is famous still thrives. ◈ *Map J4*

9 Frenaros
Archaeological finds near this village suggest that people have lived here for 10,000 years, making it one of the oldest settlements in Europe. ◈ *Map J4*

10 Potamos Liopetriou
The tiny fishing port of Liopetriou has wooden boats moored along the banks.

Sign up for DK's email newsletter on traveldk.com

Left **Fig Tree Bay** Right **Nissi Beach**

TOP10 Beaches

Mackenzie Beach, Larnaka
Mackenzie (sometimes spelt Makenzy) Beach reportedly owes its name to a Scots caterer who set up a restaurant-bar here just after World War II. Whatever the origins, this is urban Larnaka's handy beach getaway, much favoured by local families for its grey but clean sand and shallow waters. Lifeguards keep an eye on things, and date palms line the esplanade behind. ✆ Map G5

Finikoudes, Larnaka
Handy for the sights of central Larnaka, Finikoudes, with its palm-lined pedestrian esplanade, is the ideal place for a cooling swim after a morning's shopping and sightseeing. Very clean for a city beach, it has Blue Flag status and a rank of sun-loungers and umbrellas. ✆ Map G5

Agia Thekla, Agia Napa
This tiny cove west of Agia Napa manages to avoid the worst of the summer crowds. There's a small sandy beach guarded by a little white chapel. ✆ Map J4

Makronissos, Agia Napa
Makronissos's sandy hinterland is perfect for cross-country quad-biking. You can rent bikes at the beach (see p13). ✆ Map J4

Nissi Beach, Agia Napa
Sleep off the effects of a night's clubbing in the sun at Agia Napa's most favoured beach or, if you still have the energy, go waterskiing, windsurfing, para-scending or jet skiing. Bungee jumping is another popular activity here. ✆ Map J4

Kryo Nero, Agia Napa
Kryo Nero, past Agia Napa's eastern outskirts, marks the end of the long sandy stretch that begins at Limnaki. A little further along the coast are the spectacular sea caves (Thalassines Spilies), where waves have carved grottoes and arches out of the limestone cliffs. ✆ Map J4

Konnos
Pine woods cover the steep slopes behind this minute cove, hemmed in by craggy headlands. It is easiest to get to by boat, and it's a popular stop on day-trips from Protaras and Agia Napa, with good visibility for snorkelling. ✆ Map J4

Fig Tree Bay, Protaras
This crescent of sand, lapped by turquoise waves, is delightful. There is a full menu of watersports. ✆ Map J4

Protaras
Here the water is beautiful, and the soft white sand is clean and plentiful (see p69).

Louma, Pernera
Only a handful of adventurers and those in the know make it to this sandy stretch of coast, so if you want to escape the crowds, this is one to head for. ✆ Map J4

Around Cyprus – Southeast Cyprus

75

Left **Agia Napa at night** Right **The Globe**

Bars and Pubs

Bikini Bar, Protaras
You will hear the latest Greek and international hits here, a popular haunt with local twenty-somethings and visitors alike. Famed for its *café frappé*.
🅢 *Amfitritis 9 • Map J4*

Guru Ethnic Bar, Agia Napa
Guru is more stylish than the run of Agia Napa's pubs and bars – they even have a smart-casual dress code. There are three bars, bar snacks and a generally civilized atmosphere.
🅢 *Odysseos Elytis 11 • Map J4*

Sydney Australian Bar, Agia Napa
This Aussie-run pub offers the cheapest beer in Agia Napa. A stone's throw from Kryo Nero beach, it's a great place to chill during the heat of the afternoon, and gets lively after sundown.
🅢 *Kryou Nerou • Map J4*

Luke Kelly's Irish Pub, Agia Napa
Guinness on tap, and the array of paraphernalia and bonhomie that characterizes Irish pubs around the world, are all on offer here. Gets very crowded. 🅢 *Agia Mavris 28 • Map J4*

Fans, Agia Napa
The top bar for sporting action, with big-screen TVs showing the world's major sports events, from Grand Prix motor-racing to World Cup soccer.
🅢 *Archiepiskopou Makariou • Map J4*

The Bedrock Inn, Agia Napa
A colossal Fred Flintstone effigy towers over this loud caveman-themed bar, with karaoke every summer evening. Not for the faint-hearted or style conscious.
🅢 *Agios Mavris • Map J4*

Freedom Reggae Bar, Agia Napa
The gentle pulse of dub and reggae is the order of the day here. Friendly, laid-back and open day and night. 🅢 *Aris Veliochoutis • Map J4*

The Globe, Larnaka
This slightly retro expatriate hangout tries its best to recreate an authentic English pub, with a choice of keg and bottled beers, live sports TV and middle-of-the-road live bands. Open daytime and evenings. 🅢 *Evanthias Pieridou 37 • Map M5*

Marco Polo Wine Bar, Larnaka
Despite the name, Marco Polo also serves beer and is a comfortable spot to relax while checking your e-mail at one of the Internet tables. 🅢 *Athinon 10 • Map M5*

The Queen's Arms, Larnaka
A long-standing British favourite with a "buy one, get one free" happy hour from 6:30–9:30pm. Beer and stout on tap, big-screen TV, and it welcomes families with kids. 🅢 *Larnaka-Dekelia Rd • Map G5*

Left **Carwash** Right **Black and White**

TOP10 Nightspots

Carwash, Agia Napa
Unlike many of its rivals on the Agia Napa nightlife scene, Carwash stays open all year round. It also sticks to a policy of playing only dance music from the 1970s and 1980s. ✆ *Agias Mavris 24 • Map J4*

Black and White, Agia Napa
With a pronounced taste for classic soul and R&B, this small, crowded club is another Agia Napa institution. ✆ *Louka Louka 16 • Map J4*

Castle, Agia Napa
A huge club with three indoor rooms and a large dance floor outside, with music played by top international DJs. ✆ *Grigoris Afxentiou • Map J4*

Club Ice, Agia Napa
Famed for its R&B nights in the summer, which feature big-name DJs from the UK and elsewhere, this is one of the hottest places in Cyprus for R&B and garage music. An added attraction are the foam and popcorn parties. ✆ *Louka Louka 10 • Map J4*

River Reggae Club, Agia Napa
The last place to close in Agia Napa, the River Reggae Club stays open until 7am. Take a pre-dawn swim in the pool before watching the sun rise. ✆ *Belloyiannis • Map J4*

Insomnia, Agia Napa
Just when everywhere else is thinking about closing – around 4am – Insomnia opens, and plays garage music until sunrise. ✆ *Nissi 4 • Map J4*

Circus, Larnaka
Larnaka's nightlife is less Brit-oriented than Agia Napa's and Circus is no exception. With a strong local audience, its music embraces Greek pop and rock as well as mainstream dance. ✆ *Grigoris Afxentiou 17 • Map L4*

Corridor, Larnaka
A local favourite, stylish Corridor closes for the summer, then re-opens in late September for a 20- to 30-something crowd. ✆ *Karaolis 8 • Map M5*

The Edge, Larnaka
The largest nightlife complex in the Larnaka area has room for up to 2,000 people. Its beach restaurant and bar are open during the day; it hosts karaoke nights; imports live acts from the UK; and is one of the few nightspots in Cyprus to have gay nights (weekends after 11pm). ✆ *Larnaka-Dekelia Rd • Map G5*

Encounters, Larnaka
Formerly Memphis, this redesigned venue houses two clubs: Topaz with progressive, funky house music, and Deep, where the sounds are more mainstream R&B plus Greek hits. ✆ *Finikoudes promenade • Map M5*

Left **Times** Right **Express Café**

Cafés

Aragma Café, Agia Napa
Sit outdoors and watch the world of Agia Napa's harbour go by at this stylish café in the pedestrianized area by the port. Open day and night, Aragma serves coffee, bottled beers, soft drinks and cocktails, as well as a choice of sandwiches and snacks. ⊗ *Plateia Limanaki* • *Map J4*

Express Café, Agia Napa
The largest and best of an array of cafés on Agia Napa's main drag, Express is a popular, family-friendly place. It serves an extensive menu of snacks, soft drinks and alcoholic beverages. ⊗ *Archiepiskopou Makariou 29* • *Map J4*

Pepper Café, Agia Napa
Gleaming steel and zinc mark Pepper out as one of Agia Napa's most style-conscious café-bars, with outdoor tables. Mirror shades are *de rigueur*. ⊗ *Archiepiskopou Makariou* • *Map J4*

Intencity, Agia Napa
One of a chain of Internet cafés, Intencity is also noisy with the sound of gaming machines. ⊗ *Belloyiannis 10* • *Map J4*

The Blarney Stone, Larnaka
Irish coffee, Irish whisky and, of course, Guinness. For confirmed tea drinkers, the Blarney Stone also makes an excellent pot. A daytime spot rather than a night-owl's hangout. ⊗ *Kition Building Kition* • *Map G5*

Déjà vu, Larnaka
Open all day, this beachfront cafe, with framed are prints on its inside walls, is a perfect place for relaxation. It becomes a trendy lounge bar playing chill-out and ethnic sounds in the evening. ⊗ *Finikoudes promenade* • *Map M5*

Teatro Café, Larnaka
Try your hand at back-gammon, Cyprus's favourite board game, in this cheery café, while enjoying what the owner claims is the best *cappuccino* in Larnaka. ⊗ *Plateia Agiou Lazarou* • *Map M6*

Pralina, Larnaka
Pralina attracts a youthful crowd of locals, who wear a lot of black and spend as much time on their mobile phones as they do talking to each other. A great place to soak up the vibe of modern Cypriot life. ⊗ *Grigori Afxentiou* • *Map M5*

Replay, Larnaka
This Internet café on the waterfront also serves drinks. ⊗ *Finikoudes promenade* • *Map M5*

Times, Larnaka
Trendy and ultra-stylish (with plasma TVs and lively décor), this café facing the sea is popular with both young locals and discerning visitors. Fabulous coffees and great service are among the attractions. ⊗ *Finikoudes promenade* • *Map M5*

Price Categories		
For a three-course	€	€10–€15
meal for one with half	€€	€15–€25
a bottle of wine (or	€€€	€25–€35
equivalent meal), taxes	€€€€	€35–€50
and extra charges.	€€€€€	over €50

Above **Vassos Fish Harbour Restaurant**

🔟 Restaurants

Vassos Fish Harbour Restaurant, Agia Napa

A super eating place beside Agia Napa's harbour, where there's always something to watch while you eat (including the restaurant's pet pelican). The grilled fish is the best in Agia Napa and the seafood *meze* is a treat.
◈ Liminaki • Map J4 • 23 72 18 84 • Dis. access • €€€€

Palazzo Bianco, Agia Napa

Palazzo Bianco's pizza and pasta will set you up for a heavy night's partying. ◈ Aris Velouchiotis 8 • Map J4 • 23 72 19 42 • €€

Spartiatis, Agia Napa

The seafood *meze* here is made with the freshest of ingredients and beautifully presented. A good choice of Cypriot wines too. ◈ Konnou 79 • Map J4 • 23 83 13 86 • Dis. access • €€€

Limelight Taverna, Agia Napa

Booking is essential at Agia Napa's most traditional *taverna*. The best dishes come from the charcoal grill: pork, lamb, steak, lobster and fresh fish. ◈ Dionysiou Solomou 10 • Map J4 • 23 72 16 50 • €€

Marquis de Napa, Agia Napa

Everything from pizza to steak and chips, as well as Cypriot favourites and a reasonable selection for vegetarians. ◈ Kryou Nerou 22 • Map J4 • 23 72 36 10 • Dis. access • €€

Monte Carlo, Larnaka

The best tables here are on the seaside terrace, which juts out into the water. Monte Carlo's *meze* is among the most generous, and their *moussaka* also comes highly recommended. ◈ Piyale Pasha 28 • Map M6 • 24 65 38 15 • Dis. access • €€€

Krateon, Larnaka

Reservations are compulsory at Larnaka's smartest restaurant. The menu is French, and so is the ambience within this stylish old mansion with high ceilings and restrained decor. The ideal venue for a romantic holiday dinner. ◈ Kimonos 21 • Map M5 • 24 62 20 62 • Dis. access • €€€€€

Pyla Fish Tavern, Larnaka

Mouthwatering seafood at this long-established restaurant includes prawns, octopus, squid, sea bass and swordfish and much more. ◈ Frenaritis Complex Dekelia-Larnaka Rd • Map G5 • 24 64 59 90 • Dis. access • €€€€

Ambelos, Livadia

Taverna-eating at its best, in an old village house with a terrace draped with vines. A good choice of charcoal-grilled dishes, *meze* and local wines. ◈ Map G4 • 24 63 46 42 • €€€

Tochni Taverna, Tochni

The terrace here has pretty views over the valley, and there's a small pool if you want a pre-meal dip. ◈ Map E5 • 24 33 27 32 • €€

Note: Unless otherwise stated, all restaurants accept credit cards and serve vegetarian meals

Left **Akamas Peninsula** Right **Pafos harbour**

Southwest Cyprus

HOME TO ONE OF THE MOST COSMOPOLITAN CITIES, *the most up-market resort town, a stunning World Heritage Site that reveals traces of a vanished world, vineyards and mountain villages, beaches and wild coasts, southwest Cyprus is the island's most varied region. Limassol and Pafos are lively resorts, with nightlife and activities to match all tastes and a reputation for some of the Mediterranean's best resort hotels, while, wherever you look, there are visible remnants of history, from the Hellenistic mosaics of Kato Pafos to the grand amphitheatre of Kourion and the medieval fortress at Kolossi.*

Sights

1. Ancient Amathous
2. Historic Limassol
3. Limassol Folk Art Museum
4. Carob Museum, Limassol
5. Fasouri Watermania Waterpark
6. Kolossi Castle
7. Kourion
8. Sanctuary of Apollo Ylatis
9. Pafos
10. Akamas Peninsula

Archaeological Museum, Pafos

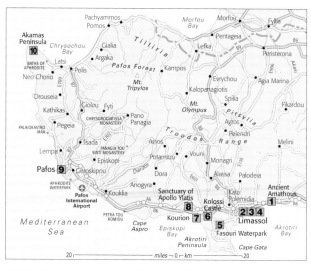

Share your travel recommendations on traveldk.com

Ancient Amathous

Ancient Amathous
Standing aloof above the coastal highway east of Limassol, the ruined foundations of Amathous can only hint of its bygone glories. This was one of the very first of the island's city-states – under the Romans it was a provincial capital, while under the Byzantine Empire it was the seat of one of the island's bishops. The remnants of an early Christian basilica, a pagan temple and a spacious Hellenistic agora (marketplace) are the highlights of a site that, despite its accessibility, not far from the luxury resorts and beaches of Limassol's tourist area, is almost always crowd-free (see pp16–17).

Historic Limassol
Behind Limassol's water-front, where newly planted palms nod in the Mediterranean breeze in front of modern high-rise buildings, lies an historic city of old-fashioned workshops and markets. Around the bulk of Limassol Castle, built by the island's medieval Lusignan dynasty, are the slender minarets of mosques built in the city's Ottoman heyday, Byzantine churches, narrow shopping streets and a plethora of cafés, bars and restaurants to suit every taste. The medieval museum, within the castle, is a must-see, with its suits of armour and ferocious weaponry, and there are great rooftop views from the castle battle-ments. The recently refurbished Central Market, in a graceful arcaded building dating from the British era in the early 20th century, is a great place to shop for handmade reed baskets, olive oil, loukoumi (Turkish delight) and other Cypriot delicacies. It is surrounded by old tavernas that make a change from the modern eating-places in the city's resort area (see pp18–19).

Limassol Municipal Folk Art Museum
Housed in a grandiose old merchant's mansion, this museum's collection is almost reminiscent of a jumble sale or an antiques shop. There is an eclectic assemblage of old wooden farm tools and house-hold utensils. There are also silver necklaces and bangles, and decorative, elaborately embroid-ered and flounced costumes that only a generation ago local women would have taken out of mothballs on village feast days and special family occasions. A wonderful insight into traditional Cypriot lifestyles (see p19).

Central market, Limassol

Limassol is also known as Lemesos

Carob Museum, Limassol

Close to the Medieval castle, the Carob museum is located in a former mill built in 1900. The exhibits clearly show how the carob is harvested, what the fruit is used for and why it has long been an important export for the island. Original machinery used to store and process the fruit and utensils are displayed, along with information panels explaining how they were used. The carob has many uses and its pods are a significant source of sugar. The fruit can be found in honey, sweets and chocolate, while its derivatives are used for making paper, photographic film plates and medicines. ◎ *Vasilissis 1 (by Limassol Castle) • Map D6 • Open May–Oct: 10am–8pm daily; Nov–Apr: 9am–5pm daily • Adm*

Fasouri Watermania Waterpark

With its high-speed chutes and slides, interactive games, pools for grown-ups, teens, sub-teens and toddlers, Cyprus's largest and most exciting waterpark offers full-on family fun. A very welcome relief from the often blistering heat of high summer, and there are restaurants and shops on site too *(see p52)*. ◎ *Lanitis Fasouri Plantations, Fasouri, Limassol • Map D6 • Open May–Oct: 10am–6pm daily • Adm*

Kolossi Castle

Kolossi Castle

Kolossi is no fairy-tale fantasy castle, but a solid, forbidding fortress which bears testimony to the military skills of its medieval builders. For a while, it was a stronghold of the piratical Knights of the Order of St John, and was surrounded by the vineyards from which they made the celebrated sweet wine, Commandaria, which was named after their "commandarie". Sacked by Genoese marauders in the 15th century, it retains many of its original features from that period, thanks to a careful restoration in the 1930s, including a private apartment and a coat of arms of one of the commanders. There are great views of the coast from the castle turrets. ◎ *14 km (9 miles) west of Limassol • Map D6 • Open Jun–Aug: 9am–7:30pm daily; Nov–Mar: 9am–5pm daily; Apr, May, Sep & Oct: 9am–6pm daily • Adm*

Kourion

Tier after tier of stone benches, able to seat up to 3,500 spectators, rise above the circular floor of Kourion's amphi-theatre, where gladia-tors and wild beasts are depicted on a well-preserved mosaic. These days,

Kourion amphitheatre

Kourion is also known as Curium

the restored theatre is the summer venue for more humane cultural events, including Cyprus's annual theatre, jazz and classical music festivals (see p58). Kourion's builders must have had an eye for landscape, too, for the theatre has fantastic views over the coast, vineyards and wheat fields of the Akrotiri Peninsula from its position 80 m (260 ft) above sea level (see pp20–21).

Sanctuary of Apollo Ylatis

Stone fragments and toppled columns mark the site of this 7th century BC shrine to the sun-god Apollo in his role as "Ylatis", or god of the woods and forests. It is one of many examples of the way in which Cyprus blended the deities of each new religion that came to the island with the cults that were already established. The site has been partially restored by archaeologists and treasures found here are on display in the island's museums. ◈ Limassol-Episkopi road, 3 km (2 miles) west of Kourion • Map C6 • Open daily. Jun–Aug: 9am–7:30pm; Nov–Mar: 9am–5pm; Apr, May, Sep & Oct: 9am–6pm • Adm

Sanctuary of Apollo Hylates

A Morning in Pafos

Start the day in Ktima, or upper Pafos, with a visit to the **Covered Market** (see p91), where you'll find lace, embroidery, ceramics and leather goods on sale and an array of open-air stalls selling everything the Cypriot housewife could wish for, from kebab skewers to fresh fruit and vegetables. From here, walk up to the town's only relic of its Ottoman past, the Cami Kebir (Grand Mosque), standing desolate and padlocked in the heart of Ktima's oldest quarter.

A stroll back along Makariou, Ktima's main street, takes you through the Central Park with its fountains and cafés to the unassuming Ethnographical Museum and, within sight of it, the much more imposing Byzantine Museum, guarded by a bust of Archbishop Makarios. The highlight of its collection is the icon of Agia Marina, dating from the 8th century AD – one of the oldest in the world.

To avoid a long, hot walk, return to the taxi stand on the town's main square, close to the corner of Makariou and Evagora Pallikaridi streets, and take a five-minute ride to view the Archaeological Museum's collection, which spans the millennia between the Bronze Age and the Byzantine era. Then, having whetted your appetite for ancient arcana, take another cab to **Kato Pafos** (see pp24–5) to see the preserved mosaics of this Roman villa complex.

Continue the Roman theme with lunch at the **Roman Restaurant** (see p95).

Pafos

Pafos is really two towns in one – Kato ("lower") Pafos and Ktima ("upper Pafos"). Kato Pafos was one of the island's most important seaports during the Middle Ages, then fell into decline and languished for centuries until tourism and the rediscovery of its famed mosaics turned it into a burgeoning resort town. Today, luxury hotels spread along the coast, east to west, and a modern centre is packed with souvenir shops, bars, cafés, nightspots and restaurants. Ktima, only 3 km (2 miles) inland, seems a world away from the tourist hype, being traditionally Cypriot, with authentic cafés and *tavernas* that cater to local tastes. Three museums in Ktima – ethnographical, archaeological and Byzantine – are well worth making time to see, each reflecting different eras on the island. Midway between the two are the eerie Tombs of the Kings, carved into a rocky hillside. Wealthy residents of the ancient city were entombed in these stone chambers from around the

Byzantine museum, Pafos

3rd century. Despite their name, there's no evidence that Pafian royalty is buried here *(see pp24–5)*. ◉ Tombs of the Kings: Tafi ton Vasileon; Map A5; Open Jun–Aug: 8am–7:30pm daily (to 6pm Apr, May, Sep & Oct; to 5pm Nov–Mar); Adm • Pafos Ethnographical Museum: Exo Vrisis 1; Map A5; Open 9:30am–5pm Mon–Sat, 10am–2pm Sun; Adm • Pafos Byzantine Museum: Andrea Ioannou 5; Map A5; Open 9am–4pm Mon–Fri, 9am–1pm Sat; Adm • Pafos Archaeological Museum: Griva Digeni; Map A5; Open 9am–5pm Mon–Fri, 10am–1pm Sat; Adm

Akamas Peninsula

The Akamas Peninsula is a beachcomber's heaven. A four-wheel drive vehicle is needed to reach this rugged spine of hills, covered with pine and juniper trees, but it's worth the effort. Along its south shore are southern Cyprus's only empty beaches, while from its western-most tip are fine coastal views. There's excellent snorkelling off its rocky shores, while divers favour the offshore islets, such as St George's Island *(see p44)*. For something less energetic, boat trips are possible from Pafos and Latsi *(see pp26–7)*.

Left **Aphrodite Waterpark** Right **Chrysorogiatissa Monastery**

🔟 Best of the Rest

Alassa Park
This green oasis, with an aviary and flock of peacocks, makes a pleasant change from busy Limassol. ◈ *Map D6 • Open 8am–8pm Tue–Sun • Dis. access • Free*

Akrotiri Peninsula
The peninsula's salt lake is a refuge in winter for bright pink flamingoes and other migrant birds. ◈ *Map D6*

Vouni Donkey Sanctuary
Vouni is a half-deserted spot whose old-fashioned houses have earned it conservation-area status. The sanctuary at Stena, just outside the village, gives a retirement home to more than 100 donkeys. ◈ *Map C5 • Open 10am–4pm Mon–Sat • Adm*

Chrysorogiatissa Monastery
This monastery produces some of the island's best wines. Within is a museum of religious paraphernalia. ◈ *Map B4 • Open 9:30am–12:30pm daily; May–Aug: 1:30–6:30pm daily; Sep–Apr: 1:30–4pm daily • Adm*

Panagia tou Sinti
The former monastery was left to crumble after the Venetians were driven from Cyprus by the Ottomans, but it underwent restoration in 1997. ◈ *Pentalia • Map B5 • Open 24 hrs daily • Free*

Aphrodite Waterpark
This visitor attraction has dozens of different thrills, spills, chutes and pools *(see p53)*. ◈ *Riccos beach, Geroskipou • Map A5 • Open 10:30am–5pm daily • Adm*

Maa
Maa is believed to be the first Greek-Mycenaean settlement in Cyprus. At the small museum weapons, amulets and jewellery are on display. ◈ *Map A5 • Mycenaean Museum: Open 10am–1pm Mon–Sat; Adm*

Lempa Neolithic Village
Primitive round-houses have been excavated by archaeologists on the site of a chalkolithic settlement. ◈ *Map A5*

Baths of Aphrodite
Hidden away in a tiny valley is the goddess's mythical bathing pool. Around the spring is a network of walking trails. ◈ *Map A4*

Polis
A combination of farming village and low-key resort, Polis has an uncrowded beach and a small seaport, Latsi, with fish tavernas. ◈ *Map A4*

⮕ *Following pages:* **Aphrodite's birthplace***

Left **Pissouri Bay** Right **Coral Bay**

Popular Beaches

Chrysochou Bay, Polis
A beautiful strip of clean pebbles and coarse sand, with clear water and great coastal views. In a forest of eucalyptus trees immediately behind the beach there's a pleasant camp site and a beach bar and restaurant. ⊗ *Map A4*

Coral Bay
This sandy crescent draws the crowds, especially on summer weekends when it is a magnet for young Cypriots. Turn up early to be sure of finding an empty sun-lounger or a patch of unoccupied sand. ⊗ *Map A5*

Pafos
Pafos municipality has transformed an unpromising stretch of shore opposite the harbour by planting lawns and palm trees, importing extra sand, providing sun-loungers, installing a beach bar, and offering an assortment of watersports. ⊗ *Map A5*

Geroskipou
This long beach on the outskirts of Pafos is little used by holidaymakers but is a favourite with locals. It is clean and well tended, and the self-service snack bar has showers, toilets and changing rooms. ⊗ *Map A5*

Pissouri Bay
Clear blue water, clean sand and pebbles, sun-loungers and umbrellas to rent, and a good choice of watersports. ⊗ *Map C6*

Evdimou
One of the least crowded and least visited beaches on the south coast. With around 2 km (1.5 miles) of sand and pebbles, it is great for beachcombers looking for solitude. A bar-restaurant midway along serves meals and cold drinks. ⊗ *Map C6*

Lady's Mile
Purportedly named after a colonial cavalry officer's favourite mare, this long stretch of gently shelving sand only a short drive from Limassol is surprisingly undeveloped, with just one small restaurant-bar which also rents out sun-loungers. ⊗ *Map D6*

Dasoudi
The nearest stretch of clean sand and water to central Limassol and justifiably popular with local urbanites as well as holidaymakers. ⊗ *Map D6*

Agios Georgios Alamanou
A natural amphitheatre of white limestone cliffs conceals this rugged stretch of shoreline from the south coast highway. The pebbles make it better suited for a quick dip before lunch than a full day's sunbathing. ⊗ *Map E6*

Governor's Beach
Dazzlingly white chalk cliffs provide a sharp contrast to the dark sands of this chain of little bays and coves, each with a choice of snack bars and tavernas. ⊗ *Map E6*

Left **Latsi** Right **Kato Pyrgos**

🔟 Hideaway Beaches

Kato Pyrgos
Close to the "Green Line" and the Turkish enclave at Kokkina, Kato Pyrgos is an adequate expanse of sand and pebbles. The hills of Tillyria form a dramatic backdrop and there are a number of places to stay and eat in the nearby village. ✎ Map C3

Mansoura
Another little-visited beach, with just one small beach bar and an admirable lack of visitors and noisy watersports to disturb its tranquillity. ✎ Map B3

Pachyammos
Pachyammos, or "Thick Sand", is aptly named. Although it can be too exposed for comfort when a north wind is blowing it is uncrowded and a fine spot for beachcombing. ✎ Map B3

Pomos
Low limestone cliffs shelter the sandy coves at Pomos, which remains happily undiscovered by the holiday industry. The water is clean, and with an archipelago of small crags and skerries just offshore it's a great place for snorkelling. ✎ Map B3

Latsi
This tiny fishing haven served as the seaport of nearby Polis in bygone days, but is beginning to be discovered by holidaymakers, with a scattering of small hotels and *tavernas* on the harbour and along the sand. ✎ Map A4

Asprokremos
Some say this is the best beach in Cyprus, and it is certainly one of the least crowded, despite its majestic sweep of sand from which you can gaze out over the sparkling, calm waters or watch splendid sunsets over Cape Amaoutis and its offshore islets. ✎ Map A4

Takkas
Sharing the bay with Asprokremos, Takkas is also overlooked by pine-covered slopes and is the perfect spot for a cooling plunge. ✎ Map A3

Fontana Amorosa
The 6-km (4-mile) walk from the Baths of Aphrodite *(see p27)* winds along rocky slopes to end near a small spring, below which this bay of sand and pebbles is a very welcome sight. ✎ Map A3

Lara Bay
This half-moon stretch to the north of Cape Lara is backed by high dunes and has fine white sand which attracts rare green and loggerhead turtles who lay their eggs here each summer *(see p26)*. ✎ Map A4

Toxeftra
Wild and empty Toxeftra lies south of Cape Lara. It's a long, straight expanse of pebbles which slopes gently into the sea. Just inland, the Avakas gorge opens onto the coast, offering pleasant walks. ✎ Map A4

Around Cyprus – Southwest Cyprus

Share your travel recommendations on traveldk.com

Left **Geroskipou** Right **Village men, Vasa**

TOP 10 Picturesque Villages

Geroskipou
Colourful shops selling traditional baskets, ceramics and the celebrated regional *loukoumi* (Turkish Delight) line the main street of this village on the outskirts of Pafos. On the south side of the main square is the five-domed church of Agia Paraskevi, inside which are religious murals dating from the 9th century.
🔍 *Map A5 • Agia Paraskevi: Open dawn–dusk daily; Dis. access; Free*

Pegeia
Pegeia's buildings are set among fields and farmland inland of Coral Bay *(see p88)*. Between the cobbled central square, with its fountains, and the former fishing harbour are foundations of two early Christian churches, with fine mosaic floors. 🔍 *Map A4*

Kathikas
Set amid chalk hills and vineyards, Kathikas is a laid-back farming village that, although close to bustling Pafos, has remained immune to tourism. Five minutes' drive from the centre, the Sterna Winery is open for tastings *(see p56)*. 🔍 *Map A4*

Pissouri
A hilltop location above a beach lapped by clear blue water makes Pissouri one of the most sought-after addresses on the south coast for expats. A great combination of peace and quiet, choice of places to eat and drink, and low-key nightlife. 🔍 *Map C6*

Potamiou
Tumbledown old houses with overhanging balconies grace the narrow streets of this village in the Troodos foothills. 🔍 *Map C5*

Vasa
Expats and Cypriot urbanites have snapped up many of the delightful cottages in this wine-growing village, but it still has a character all its own. 🔍 *Map C5*

Drouseia
Overlooked by the limestone crags of Agios Georgios, Drouseia is one of the region's prettiest villages, with graceful old stone houses standing above steep lanes. 🔍 *Map A4*

Malia
The crumbling minarets of mosques that have remained unused since their Turkish Cypriot faithful fled in 1974 lend this half-deserted village a melancholy ambience. 🔍 *Map C5*

Arsos
The largest of the wine-making villages is a mellow community of sturdy old stone buildings. 🔍 *Map C5*

Dora
Within the church of Panagia Fotolampousa, on a hillside above this tiny village, is an antique icon of the Virgin which must, according to Christian Orthodox tradition, remain veiled forever. 🔍 *Map C5*

Left **Covered market, Ktima Pafos** Right **Panagia's Souvenir Market, Geroskipou**

🔟 Places to Shop

1 The Inside Story, Kato Polemidia
A great place to find antique ceramics, earthenware pottery, brass lamps and old photographs. Just outside central Limassol, at Kato Polemidia. ✆ *Corner of Euripidou and Akademou • Map D6*

2 Panagia's Souvenir Market, Geroskipou
You can't miss Panagia Athinodorou's colourful shop on the north side of the central square, with its array of bright-painted pottery, colourful *tsestos* (bread trays) and cane baskets. ✆ *Makarios 23 • Map A5*

3 Phoebe Mosaic Workshop, Lania
Specializing in colourful mosaics, both copies of famous ancient works and modern originals. They can arrange for larger items to be shipped to home. ✆ *Map C5*

4 Steptoe's of Chlorakas
More a glorified junk shop than an antiques store, Steptoe's is worth foraging through for treasures to take home. The stock changes constantly, though judging by the patina of age on some items they may have languished unsold for years. ✆ *Map A5*

5 The Antique Mart, Limassol
The English owner searches out antique furniture and other collectables from all over Cyprus. ✆ *Agiou Andreou 277 • Map D6*

6 The Wine Jar, Limassol
For local souvenirs, look no further than this tourist-orientated store. ✆ *Promachon Eleutherias • Map D6*

7 Cyprus Handicraft Centre, Limassol & Pafos
Two government-run stores specialize in island crafts such as Lefkara lace. ✆ *Limassol: Themidos 25; Map D6 • Pafos:Apostolou Pavlou 64;Map A5*

8 Splendido, Limassol
Children will love the hand-made dolls here, some of which are dressed in traditional costumes. ✆ *Agiou Andreou 209 • Map D6*

9 Mikis Antiques, Ktima Pafos
The place to find old wind-up gramophones and musical instruments. ✆ *Fellahoglou 6 • Map A5*

10 Covered Market, Ktima Pafos
A selection of stalls selling lace, embroidery, handmade leather bags, beachwear and other souvenirs. ✆ *Agoras • Map A5*

Mikis Antiques, Ktima Pafos

 There are also Cyprus Handicraft Centres in Larnaca and Nicosia, and all guarantee that their goods are authentic products

Left **The Basement** Right **Privilege**

TOP 10 Nightspots

The Basement, Limassol
Georgiou 1 (marked on some maps as Georgiou A) is Limassol's prime party hotspot. This tiny place is usually jammed with young locals and visitors; the music is mainstream pop and rock. ◈ *Georgiou 1 • Map D6*

Sesto Senso, Limassol
One of the most popular venues not only in Limassol but the whole of Cyprus. The classy décor and up-to-date Greek and international chart sounds keep its clientele happy all the year round. ◈ *Georgiou 1 • Map D6*

The Half Note, Limassol
The Half Note hosts the occasional live band but its main stock-in-trade is Latin music. It attracts a dedicated local crowd every Friday and Saturday night – turn up early to be sure of getting in. ◈ *Socratous 4 • Map D6*

Prime, Limassol
Formerly known as The Hippodrome, this sizeable venue is very popular with clubbers of all ages. Good light show and a friendly laid-back atmosphere. ◈ *Georgiou 1 • Map D6*

Privilege, Limassol
This huge venue is out of the tourist area but is worth the taxi fare. The music is a mix of European and Greek chart hits, with a choice of dancing spaces. ◈ *Off the Limassol-Nicosia Rd, 3 km (2 miles) east of Amathous • Map E6*

The Gallery, Pafos
Come here for an evening of garage and R&B in this lively, friendly club that is a well-established favourite. ◈ *Agiou Antoniou • Map A5*

Rainbow, Pafos
You can't miss Rainbow, which flaunts its neon sign above Pafos's "nightlife street", Agiou Antoniou. It's the resort's longest established nightspot, with a musical menu that rivals anything in Agia Napa or even Ibiza, and guest DJs from the UK, Germany and the Netherlands. ◈ *Agiou Antoniou • Map A5*

Barrio del Mar, Pafos
A huge summer venue with indoor and outdoor facilities. There are no fewer than six bars, while the varied music programme ensures the place is packed. ◈ *Geroskipou Beach • Map A5*

Starsky & Hutch, Pafos
The name gives it away really – tunes of the 1970s and 80s alternate with the latest club, garage and R&B sounds. ◈ *Agiou Antoniou • Map A5*

Cartel Seaside, Pafos
One of the newest additions to the Pafos nightlife scene, this is a café that turns into a club at night. Popular all the year round, the music becomes more international as the summer goes on. Great atmosphere. ◈ *Poseidonos, Kato Pafos • Map A5*

Left **Café Vienna** Right **Woody'z**

🔟 Bars, Pubs and Cafés

Galatex Complex, Limassol

You'll find eight bars for the price of one in this drinker's paradise so bring a man-sized thirst with you. There is something for everyone here, from the Down-under Sports Bar with big-screen sporting action to the Red Lion Pub serving English beers on tap. ◈ *Georgiou 1 • Map D6*

Graffiti Lounge, Limassol

Style-conscious Graffiti attracts few foreign visitors, perhaps because it's in the town centre rather than in the tourist area. It offers relaxed background music, a good choice of drinks, and hookah pipes for those who like their tobacco Middle Eastern-style. ◈ *Agiou Andreou 23C • Map D6*

Roadhouse Pub, Limassol

The Roadhouse does its best to recreate an English pub, with roast dinners on Sundays, a garden bar and live music most week nights. ◈ *Messalias 6, Germasogeia • Map D6*

Step Inn Irish Bar, Limassol

This massive Irish pub on four floors has sports screenings on satellite TV, snooker, darts, nightly karaoke, and, of course, Guinness and other Irish beers on tap. ◈ *Georgiou 1 89 • Map D6*

The Woodman, Limassol

More decorous and family-orientated than some of its rivals, this pleasant pub-restaurant serves substantial meals. ◈ *Georgiou 1 73A • Map D6*

127, Limassol

This pleasant café-bar has tables outside in a shady garden, and serves good coffee, sandwiches, snacks and pastries. ◈ *Elenis Paleologinas 5 • Map D6*

Bubbles Cocktail Bar, Pafos

It's always party time at this loud and lively Pafos music bar, which is famous for its strong cocktails. ◈ *Agiou Antoniou • Map A5*

The Robin Hood, Pafos

This cheerfully kitsch pub with its medieval castle-style theme has a choice of cold beers on tap. ◈ *Agiou Antoniou • Map A5*

Café Vienna, Pafos

More sedate and stylish than most of Pafos's bars, Café Vienna is a shady retreat serving excellent coffee, pastries and sandwiches. ◈ *Poseidonos • Map A5*

Woody'z, Pafos

Cheerful and busy every night, Woody'z attracts a young party crowd with cocktails and some top international music. ◈ *Agiou Antoniou • Map A5*

The Robin Hood

Left **Aliada** Right **Neromilos**

🔟 Traditional Restaurants

Aliada, Limassol
The attractive garden, behind this elegant Limassol mansion, is a delightful place to dine on a summer evening, and there are also four dining rooms inside, much favoured by locals in the know. The food is some of the best in the region, especially the charcoal-grilled dishes. ◎ *Eirinis 117 • Map D6 • 25 34 07 58 • €€€*

Neon Phaliron, Limassol
Something of a local legend for its combination of traditional recipes with an up-to-date twist. Game features heavily in season, and the seafood is well worth trying too. ◎ *Gladstonos 135 • Map D6 • 25 36 57 68 • €€€*

Pasalimani, Limassol
Pasalimani, with sea views, maintains its long established reputation as one of Limassol's best fish restaurants. ◎ *Leoforos Amathountas • Map D6 • 25 32 14 94 • Dis. access • €€€€*

Xydas, Limassol
Make reservations well in advance if you want a table at Limassol's best fish taverna. ◎ *22 Anthemidos • Map D6 • 25 72 83 36 • €€*

Neromilos, Pera Pedi
A delightful village tavern, beside a chuckling stream that formerly drove the watermill. All the Cypriot favourites, prepared on the charcoal grill or in a traditional clay oven. ◎ *Anexartisias • Map C5 • 25 47 05 36 • €€*

Plaka, Pafos
Don't be fooled by Plaka's unexciting appearance – it is one of the best tavernas in Pafos. Try the lavish, multi-course seafood *meze*. ◎ *Poseidonos 65 • Map A5 • 26 96 56 14 • Dis. access • €€€*

Porto Latchi, Latsi
Near the tiny fishing harbour at Latsi, this traditional fish tavern with outdoor tables has good seafood every day, as well as *meze* and charcoal-grilled meat dishes. ◎ *Akamantos • Map A4 • 26 32 15 30 • Dis. access • €€€*

Akamas Fish Tavern, Agios Georgios
Perched above a tiny fishing harbour, this delightful restaurant serves fish, naturally, as well as excellent *meze* and kebabs. ◎ *Map A4 • 26 62 18 88 • €€€*

Seven St Georges, Pafos
Traditional Cypriot dishes are served up with a highly original, creative twist at this wonderful family-run restaurant. Dining here is a fascinating experience. ◎ *Geroskipou • Map A5 • 26 96 31 76 • Dis. access • €€*

Araouzos, Kathikas
In the heart of the wine-making country between Pafos and the north coast, Araouzos is a gem of a restaurant that amply repays the minor trouble of getting here. The menu consists of stews, game dishes and roasts. ◎ *Map A4 • 26 63 20 76 • €€€*

Price Categories

For a three-course	€	€10–€15
meal for one with half	€€	€15–€25
a bottle of wine (or	€€€	€25–€35
equivalent meal), taxes	€€€€	€35–€50
and extra charges.	€€€€€	over €50

Above **Roman Restaurant**

TOP 10 International Restaurants

1 La Maison Fleurie, Limassol

Not for those on a tight budget, this French restaurant has a claim to be the best eating place in Limassol, and perhaps Cyprus, and has received international acclaim. The menu is a gourmet's delight. ✆ *Christaki Kranou 18 • Map D6 • 25 32 06 80 • €€€€€*

2 Cleopatra, Limassol

For an exotic experience – belly dancers, hookah pipes and all – visit this fine Lebanese restaurant. The menu is authentically Middle Eastern and you can sample an after-dinner *nargileh* (hubble-bubble pipe) packed with apple-flavoured tobacco. ✆ *Christiana Court, John Kennedy • Map D6 • 25 58 67 11 • €€*

3 Barolo, Limassol

Bustling Barolo is a favourite for lunch. There's a strong Italian twist to the menu. ✆ *Agiou Andreou 248 • Map D6 • 25 76 07 67 • €€€*

4 Beige, Limassol

This modern, high-class gourmet restaurant is unique in Cyprus, combining flavours from the East with those of the Mediterranean. ✆ *Agiou Andreou 238 • Map D6 • 25 81 88 60 • €€€€€*

5 Calcutta, Limassol

An odd but inspired hybrid, Calcutta serves spicy Indian dishes and fabulous *meze*. Good choices for vegetarians too. ✆ *Georgiou A, 2 • Map D6 • 25 32 25 11 • €€*

6 Old Vienna, Limassol

Pamper your sweet tooth at this Austrian-style café, with the best and creamiest cakes and pastries in town. A tempting menu of meaty Viennese main meals is on offer too. ✆ *Kanika Enaerios Complex • Map D6 • 25 58 93 27 • €€€*

7 Roman Restaurant, Pafos

Colourfully kitsch, the Roman Hotel's poolside restaurant is decorated in an imitation of a Hellenistic villa, complete with arches, columns and painted friezes. The pool is open to visitors as well as residents. ✆ *Tafos ton Vasileon • Map A5 • 26 94 44 00 • €€€€*

8 Koh i Noor, Pafos

A varied menu of curries and tandoori dishes, prepared by Indian chefs. ✆ *Kleios 7 • Map A5 • 26 96 55 44 • €€€*

9 Chloe's Chinese Restaurant, Pafos

The best Chinese restaurant in town. For those in self-catering accommodation, they also deliver take-away orders. ✆ *Poseidonos 13 • Map A5 • 26 93 46 76 • Dis. access • €€€€*

10 Kolossi Steak House, Kolossi

This friendly place is a favourite with British armed forces families from the nearby bases as it serves English roasts. ✆ *Map D6 • 25 93 25 70 • Dis. access • €€*

Note: Unless otherwise stated, all restaurants accept credit cards and serve vegetarian meals

Left **Fresco, Troodos church** Right **View from Mount Olympus**

The Troodos Mountains

OOL, PINE-SCENTED BREEZES WAFT OVER THE FORESTED SLOPES *of the High Troodos region, making it a perfect refuge from the searing summer heat of Nicosia, and the crowded coastal areas seem like another world away. The Troodos peaks dominate the horizons of southern Cyprus, and in winter and early spring, when they are often capped with snow, they are at their most spectacular. Modern roads have made their old-fashioned villages more accessible, but there are still a great many off-road forest tracks and paths to explore on foot or on a mountain bike, and getting to some of the region's world-renowned painted churches calls for a four-wheel drive vehicle or a pair of walking boots. It is worth the effort to discover the heart of the island – a region of wildlife, wildflowers and an ancient way of life.*

 Sights

1	Troodos Painted Churches	6	Mount Olympus
2	Prodromos	7	Kakopetria
3	Trooditissa Monastery	8	Galata
4	Platres	9	Agios Ioannis Lampadistis
5	Caledonia Falls	10	Tilliria

Tilliria

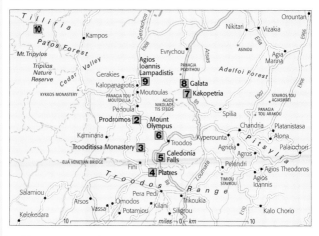

Share your travel recommendations on traveldk.com

Troodos Painted Churches

Hidden in the high valleys of the remote Troodos, these modest little churches and monastery chapels conceal a treasury of some of the most glorious early Christian works of art in the world. Miraculously, their glowing frescoes have survived the rise and fall of half a dozen empires. Some are more than 1,000 years old and in their way they inspire as much awe as any great cathedral (see pp22–3).

Prodromos

The highest settlement in Cyprus, at 1,440 m (4,725 ft) above sea level, Prodromos commands the pass between Mount Olympus in the east and Agios Ilias, in the west. It stands among cherry and apple orchards that enhance the area with their pink-and-white blooms in spring and early summer. Nearby, the artificial lake of the Prodromos reservoir attracts trout fishermen and, in spring and autumn, migrant waterfowl. ◎ Map C4

Trooditissa Monastery

A secret mountain cave and a miraculous icon of the Virgin are Trooditissa's main claims to fame. High above Platres on the Troodos mountain slopes, it was founded during the 13th century

Trooditissa Monastery

beneath a grotto where hermits, according to local legend, guarded the holy icon for many years. The cave can be visited by all, but the monastery and its wondrous icon may be seen only by Orthodox pilgrims who journey here in their droves.
◎ Map C4 • Closed to the public

Platres

Situated above a mountain stream that becomes a fierce torrent in winter and spring, Platres is the southern gateway to the Troodos ranges and the most popular spot in the region, with restaurants, souvenir shops and places to stay. It is also the ideal base for exploring the region, with walking and biking trails branching off in all directions, trout fishing available and a cool climate even in high summer. The village is divided into two districts: Pano (Upper) Platres, the main resort area, and traditional Kato (Lower) Platres. ◎ Map C5

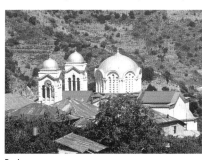

Prodromos

Icons and Frescoes

The names of almost all the artists who painted the icons and frescoes of the Troodos churches are unknown. Legends claim many of the oldest icons "flew" to Cyprus of their own accord in the 8th century to escape destruction by a purist Christian sect, the Iconoclasts ("icon breakers"). Common themes for the frescoes include the Crucifixion and Resurrection, and the Last Judgement, with halo-wearing saints and martyrs, grinning demons, crimson dragons and Roman soldiers.

Caledonia Falls

Tumbling into a wooded ravine, this beautiful 11-m (36-ft) waterfall, surrounded by forest, is at its most spectacular in spring, when the Troodos streams are fed by melting winter snow from the mountain peaks. It is most popular in summer, when it offers a cool and shady retreat from the powerful midday sun. Its name originally derives from the swallows (chelidonia) which chase flying insects above its pool on summer evenings (see p50). ✎ Map C5

Caledonia Falls

Mount Olympus

Visit the highest peak of the Troodos range for fantastic views over the mountains and down to the sea. It's a welcome breath of cool mountain air in summer and, from January to early March, a skier's delight. The 1,950-m (6,400-ft) peak shares its name with the much higher mountain that was the legendary home of Zeus and the rest of the Greek gods on mainland Greece, and with other summits in the Greek islands and Asia Minor. It is also known as Chionistra or "the snowy one" (see p50). ✎ Map C4

Kakopetria

The name of this village translates as "evil rocks" and it's not hard to see why, when one looks over the harsh surrounding landscape. Despite the ominous introduction, Kakopetria is a pretty and prosperous village and a favourite getaway spot for Nicosian city-dwellers (see p39). It is also a good base for exploring many of the remarkable Troodos painted churches nearby. ✎ Map D4

Galata

The precarious-looking balconies of handsome old village houses overhang the narrow main street of this old-fashioned community, which is about 2 km (1 mile) above Kakopetria. The village is located above a fast-flowing mountain stream. An ideal base from which to explore the nearby Troodos churches. ✎ Map D4

Agios Ioannis Lampadistis

Unique among the island's monasteries because it has changed little since its founda-tion some time during the 11th century, Agios Ioannis Lampa-distis is set beside a sacred

Kakopetria

spring and is incredibly well preserved. A riot of colourful 13th- to 15th-century frescoes, covering the walls of the three chapels that nestle together under one pitched roof, depicts much of the gospel *(see p22)*.
✎ *Map C4 • Open May–Oct: 8am–1pm, 2–6pm Tue–Sun; Nov–Apr: 8am–1pm, 2–4pm Tue–Sun • Free*

Tilliria

Cyprus's last real stretch of mountain and forest wilderness is a vast tract of pine-covered hillsides that slope down from the western flank of the Troodos range towards the beaches of the west coast. The region is criss-crossed with numerous nature trails and is one of the very few areas where attentive walkers might be lucky enough to catch a fleeting glimpse of one of the thousand or so moufflon (wild sheep) still surviving in their natural habitat. Tilliria is also a haven for a variety of birds, and in spring and autumn its woodland glades are vivid with crocus, anemones and other wild flowers. ✎ *Map C3*

A Morning Hike on Mount Olympus

🕐 Although the summit of **Mount Olympus** can be reached by car, hiking to the peak on foot offers a greater sense of achievement. Start from the Troodos resort car park and follow the signposted Atalante Trail, which is waymarked by strategically positioned red dots. Following the 1,750-m (5,750-ft) contour, this is an undemanding walk for most of the way, through pine and juniper woods, where birds and butterflies flit and with glimpses of the sea and the plains far below. Covering a little over 16 km (10 miles) and only 200 m (650 ft) in altitude, this walk can be completed in a morning by anyone of reasonable fitness, but comfortable trainers or walking boots, water and – especially in summer – a hat and sunblock are musts.

After around three hours, the so-called Atalante Trail connects with the **Artemis Trail** *(see p48)* and a detour upward to the summit (you can't miss the giant radar masts and telecom towers) then loops back down to the Troodos resort. En route you will pass mineral formations and information markers supplied by the tourist office that point out the indigenous plants and wildlife of the region.

At the summit are the ruins of a 16th-century Venetian fortress, built in a vain attempt to defend the island against the invading Ottomans.

🍴 Your walk completed, enjoy a lunch of fresh trout in **Pano Platres**.

Around Cyprus – The Troodos Mountains

⟶ *Following pages:* **Fresco, Panagia Forviotissa, Troodos**

ΓΕ
Φ
Θ

+ ΙΠ ΠΟΝ ΑΚ ΕCC Ε ΥCΟ ΒΗC ΝΗ ΓΗ ΘCΟ ΘΕΡΙΜΟCΝΟΚ
CΝ ΑΙΑ ΘΕ ΠΟΡΟ ΑΝΗCΤΕCΕCΝΟ ΜΟ CΤ Ε ΜΕΝ Α
ΕΠ ΑΜΑ ΘΕ ΙCΓ ΡΤ CΟΙΠΗ ΚΥΙΤ ΔΕ CΟΠΙ CΤ ΜΗ ΙΑ
ΗC Β Ω ΠΡΟΘΝΕ ΑΤΗΜ ΑΝΤΑΝ ΑΝΘΙ CΕ Α ΖΑΝΤΙΝΙ
Μ ΤΓ ΑΕ CΙ ΝΙ Κ Τ ΓΠ ΟCΟΥ ΚΑ ΙΜ ΟΝΤ ΟΝ
ΕΝΘ ΑΔ C

Η Π ΓΙΑ
ΑΝΑCΤΑCΙΑ

Η ΤΘΗ ΤΟ Τ CΕΛΗCΕΝ
ΤΟ ΘΑΛΜΑΤΙΚΟΝ

Left **Omodos** Right **Palaiochori**

Best of the Rest

Omodos
The main attraction here is the Timiou Stavrou monastery, believed to house fragments of the True Cross. ✪ *Map C5*

Trikoukia
The church of Panagia Trikou-kiotissa is all that remains of this monastery built in the 13th century. The church contains an icon of the Virgin which is credited with the ability to bring rain to parched fields. ✪ *Map D5*

Palaiochori
This village stands among fragrant citrus groves and fertile fields. Its Museum of Byzantine Heritage displays icons and ecclesiastical vestments. ✪ *Map D4 • Museum: Open 10am–1pm Tue & Wed; Dis. access; Adm*

Pitsylia Region
Vines, almonds and hazel-nuts are the mainstay of the these hill-farming villages. ✪ *Map D4*

Almyrolivado
The focal point of this hill-side spot is a giant juniper tree, said to be the oldest tree on the island. ✪ *Map D4*

Fini
Fini is famous for its beautiful pottery and the highlight of the village is the Pottery Museum, displaying jars, oil lamps and old kilns. ✪ *Map C5 • Museum: Open 10am–1pm daily; Adm*

Elia Venetian Bridge
This arched stone bridge – one of many in the area – crossing a stream bed is testament to the skills of the Venetians who drove a highway through these hills. Mule trains carried copper ore from the Troodos mines to the harbour at Pafos. ✪ *Map C5*

Kaminaria
On the eastern fringes of the Pafos forest, this tiny village's 19th-century church of Agios Georgios is worth a visit for its displays of ancient icons. ✪ *Map C4*

Marathassa Valley
The hill villages of Pedoulas and Moutoulas are the most convenient gateways to the dramatic Marathassa Valley, covered with cherry orchards. ✪ *Map C4*

Tomb of Makarios
Sentries keep watch around the clock outside the mountain-top tomb of Archbishop Makarios III *(see p29)*. From the summit you can see for miles across the forests. ✪ *Map C4*

Price Categories

For a three-course	€ €15–€15
meal for one with half	€€ €15–€25
a bottle of wine (or	€€€ €25–€35
equivalent meal), taxes	€€€€ €35–€50
and extra charges.	€€€€€ over €50

Above **Fyti Pefkos**

Places to Eat

1 Skylight Swimming Pool Restaurant, Platres

Just the place to cool off after a drive around the Troodos, the Skylight restaurant has its own swimming pool – free to diners, with a minimal charge for those just dropping in for a cold drink. The menu features fresh mountain trout, an array of dishes from the charcoal grill, and some decent local wines. *Map C5 • 25 42 22 44 • €€€*

2 A&J Village Taverna, Platres

This traditional *taverna* is an ideal year-round choice: in warm weather there are tables outside under a shady terrace, and in the cooler months there is a large, cosy indoor dining room. The menu runs the gamut of Cypriot dishes to grilled trout and international favourites. *Makariou 26 • Map C5 • 25 42 27 77 • €€€*

3 Psilodendro Trout Farm Restaurant

Catch your trout, then eat it at this open-air restaurant on the northern outskirts of Platres. Also serves kebabs, mixed grills and salads. *Psilodendro • Map C5 • 25 42 13 50 • €€*

4 To Anoi, Platres

A typically Cypriot hybrid of English-style pub and traditional café, with cold beer and soft drinks, kebabs and other light meals, sandwiches and ice creams on offer. *Map C5 • 25 42 29 00 • €*

5 Fyti Pefkos, Fini

Get here in time to watch the mountain sunset. All the favourite Cypriot grills and casseroles can be enjoyed here. *Map C5 • 26 73 25 70 • €*

6 Neraida, Fini

This restaurant stands beside a clear stream that flows over the waterfall above and specializes in fresh river trout. *Map C5 • 25 42 16 80 • €€*

7 Fini Tavern, Fini

A British expat's home from home, with a nostalgic 1970s-style menu of prawn cocktail, chicken Kiev and Black Forest Gâteau. *Map C5 • 25 42 18 28 • Closed Sun D, Mon • €€€€*

8 Linos Inn, Kakopetria

Old-fashioned furnishings, a leafy outdoor terrace and a menu of Cypriot standards. *Map D4 • 22 92 31 61 • Dis. access • €€€*

9 Mill Restaurant, Kakopetria

The riverside restaurant of Kakopetria's large hotel features trout and international standards. *Mill Hotel • Map D4 • 22 92 25 36 • Closed Nov–Apr • Dis. access • €€€*

10 To Vrisi, Pedoula

This *taverna* offers a truly Cypriot experience, with a menu of mountain trout, Troodos pickles, candied cherries and other regional specialities. *Map C4 • No phone • Dis. access • €€€*

Left **Kyrenia harbour** Right **Salamis**

Northern Cyprus

PALM TREES, MINARETS, MOSQUES *and the ruins of Crusader castles and great medieval abbeys built in the heyday of the Lusignans all add to Northern Cyprus's languid, Middle Eastern ambience. Quite separate from southern Cyprus, in both atmosphere and landscape as well as politics, here there are empty beaches to bask on, splendid hiking in rugged mountains with views out to sea, and small harbours where old-fashioned fishing schooners moor at quays crammed with the tables of lively fish restaurants. Here, too, are potent reminders of the North's troubled history. Abbeys and cathedrals that were forcibly converted into Muslim places of worship after the Ottoman conquest and the Orthodox churches abandoned after the 1974 invasion are all a mark of Turkish triumphalism, yet many Turkish Cypriots are eager to tell visitors of their sincere desire for reconciliation between the island's separated communities. A benefit of a visit to the North is that, as a result of the international boycott that has afflicted tourism to the North since 1974, life here proceeds at a far gentler pace than in the South.*

Karpas Peninsula

🔟 Sights

1. Northern Nicosia
2. Kyrenia
3. St Hilarion Castle
4. Bellapais Abbey
5. Buffavento Castle
6. Salamis
7. Famagusta Walled City
8. St Barnabas Monastery
9. Kantara Castle
10. Karpas Peninsula

For practical details on entering and visiting Northern Cyprus
See pp114–7

Northern Nicosia

Crumbling old houses and a cheerful clutter of bazaars surround the medieval monuments of the Turkish half of the divided city. The Selimiye Mosque – a picturesque hybrid of medieval Christian and Islamic architecture – is the city's most prominent landmark. ✎ Map F3

Kyrenia

Beneath the jagged sierra of the Kyrenia range, this city is home to a pleasant collection of shops, restaurants and hotels around and above a superb natural harbour. It is dominated by the battlements of a massive Venetian sea-fort that withstood every assault for centuries until, in 1570, its defenders surrendered to the Ottomans. The North's best hotels are found either side of the city *(see pp130–31)*. ✎ Map F2

St Hilarion Castle

Built in the 11th century for the Lusignan kings and steeped in history, St Hilarion would be the perfect setting for a medieval romance, with its elaborate defences built around steep mountain crags. Legends, indeed, surround it, including tales of a hidden treasure-room, an enchanted garden, and stories of Byzantine treachery and

St Hilarion Castle

medieval intrigue. It was last occupied in the 16th century by the Venetians. ✎ Map E3 • Open Jun–Oct: 9am–4:45pm daily; Nov–May: 9am–1pm, 2–4:45pm • Adm

Bellapais Abbey

Perched above the sea, Bellapais would be worth the journey into the mountains just for the view. But the abbey, built by the Augustinian order in 1200, is also the most spectacular piece of Gothic architecture in Cyprus, with vaulted stonework decorated with elaborate carving. ✎ Map F3 • Open Jun–Oct: 9am–4:45pm daily; Nov–May: 9am–1pm, 2–4:45pm • Adm

Bellapais Abbey

 Kyrenia is known as Girne in Turkish

Salamis

Buffavento Castle
Almost 1,000 m (3,300 ft) above sea level, Buffavento's dilapidated square tower and keep were built by the Byzantines to watch for Saracen raiders and alert the defenders of Kyrenia. Long abandoned, its windy battlements offer breathtaking views of the coast – even with no pirate sails in sight. ⍟ Map F3 • Open in summer 9am–4:45pm daily; in winter 9am–1pm, 2–4:45pm daily (hours may vary due to military occupation) • Free

History of Salamis
Salamis was first settled by Mycenaean Greeks, and by the 5th century BC it had become the most important city-state on the island. Its kings resisted the Persian empire and became allies of Alexander the Great, but after his death the city was conquered by Ptolemy I. After Christianity came to Cyprus it became once again the island's capital. A series of natural disasters in the 4th century led to its decline, and the city vanished beneath the sand. It was rediscovered by archaeologists but excavations were interrupted by the events of 1974, and more of the site remains to be unearthed.

Salamis
Graceful columns, rising from a honeycomb of toppled walls, mark the site of the greatest of Cyprus's ancient cities. Founded more than 3,000 years ago, Salamis dominated the island until its near-destruction by earthquakes in the 4th century AD. Archaeologists have found Hellenistic mosaics, the remains of Roman baths, a fine amphitheatre and the foundations of two Byzantine basilicas. ⍟ Map J3 • Open Jun–Oct: 9am–7pm daily; Nov–May: 9am–1pm, 2–4:45pm daily • Adm

Lala Mustafa Pasa Mosque, Famagusta

Famagusta Walled City
Within Venetian ramparts, Famagusta conceals a wealth of Gothic and Islamic architecture. At its heart is the Lala Mustafa Pasa Mosque, originally the cathedral of St Nicholas, with its graceful Gothic porticoes and six-paned rose window. Huge stone cannon-balls, relics of the eight-month siege of the city in 1570, lie in the streets, while overlooking the harbour is the "Othello Tower", so called because Famagusta was the main setting for Shakespeare's play. ⍟ Map J4

St Barnabas Monastery
The imposing monastery with its sturdy dome was built in 1756, but its main attraction for Orthodox pilgrims was a much

Famagusta is also known as Gazimaguza; St Barnabas Monastery is also known as Apostolos Varnavas

older relic: the tomb of St Barnabas, who brought Christianity to Cyprus. Within the monastery is an archaeological museum housing delicate Bronze Age pottery. ◈ *Map J3 • Open Jun–Oct: 9am–7pm daily; Nov–May: 9am–1pm, 2–4:45pm • Adm*

Kantara Castle

Commanding the western end of the Kyrenia range, Kantara's walls ascend from a formidable barbican gate to a ring of inner battlements and towers. When Richard the Lionheart conquered the island this was the last refuge of the Byzantine prince of Cyprus, Isaac Comnenos. ◈ *Map J2 • Open in summer 9am–5pm daily; in winter 9am–1pm, 2–4:45pm daily*

Karpas Peninsula

This long, rocky spit is the least developed part of the island, with sandy beaches on its north and south coast and a scattering of historic Christian churches, including the monastery of Apostolos Andreas, which is being restored with UN and EU funding. Within is a holy well famed for its mystic healing properties. ◈ *Map K2*

Karpas Peninsula

A Morning in Northern Nicosia

Enter **Northern Nicosia** *(see p105)* at the Kyrenia Gate and walk south down Girne Caddesi to Ataturk Meydan, the hub of the old town. South of there, the city's historic buildings tower above a maze of narrow streets.

Walk down Asmaali Sok to the fortress-like Büyük Han, a 16th-century *caravanserai* with an arcaded courtyard which now houses artists' studios, handicraft shops and a pleasant café, then turn left towards the soaring Gothic front of the Selimiye Cami. This 700-year-old cathedral of Agia Sofia (Holy Wisdom) turned mosque is Northern Nicosia's greatest glory. Behind it, signs lead you to a small square, Selimiye Meydan, and the Sultan Mahmut Library, an eight-sided building with a domed roof containing a collection of Islamic manuscripts and ancient Korans. On the opposite side of the square, a collection of stonework in the Lapidary Museum includes medieval crests, Turkish tombstones and gargoyles stripped from the Gothic cathedral.

Immediately south of the Selimiye is another Gothic relic, the church of St Nicholas, which became a storehouse under the Ottomans. Across the road, the Belidiye Pazari is the town's central market, with a colourful mix of produce stands and arts and crafts sellers.

Walk back through the Arabahmet quarter, and enjoy lunch at the **Boghjalian Konak Restaurant** *(see p111).*

Left **Kyrenia Castle** Right **Clay wine-jars, Shipwreck Museum, Kyrenia Castle**

Best of the Rest

Kyrenia Castle
Within Kyrenia Castle is the Shipwreck Museum, housing the world's oldest wrecked ship – sunk around 300 BC and salvaged in 1967 – complete with its ancient cargo of wine-jars and grindstones. Also here is the fascinating Tomb-Finds Gallery, which displays Neolithic, Bronze Age and Hellenistic treasures. ✎ *Map F2 • Open Jun–Oct: 9am–7pm daily; Nov–May: 9am–1pm, 2–4:45pm daily • Adm*

Kyrenia Decorative Arts Museum
This collection of Ottoman furniture, Oriental vases and prints of old Kyrenia is housed in a colonial villa. ✎ *Ozomer Ozocak 20 • Map F2 • Open Jun–Oct: 9am–2pm daily; Nov–May: 9am–1pm, 2–4:45pm daily • Adm*

Kyrenia Folk Art Museum
Traditional implements such as the wooden olive-oil press on display here were in use only a generation ago. ✎ *Map F2 • Open Jun–Oct: 9am–2pm daily; Nov–May: 9am–1pm, 2–4:45pm daily • Adm*

Vouni
Built around 480 BC, the royal palace's design in this village shows clear Persian influences. ✎ *Map C3*

Soloi
Mosaics of birds and animals can be seen in the basilica of this ruined 5th-century BC town. ✎ *Map C3*

Lefka
Lefka has the feel of a desert oasis town, heightened by its mosque standing alone in a grove of palm trees. ✎ *Map C3*

Antifonitis Monastery
A painted *Pantokrator* (Christ) gazes down from the dome of this 12th-century church. ✎ *Map G3 • Open 9am–1pm daily • Free*

Iskele
This town's Byzantine church is decorated with fluid frescoes. ✎ *Map J3 • Panagia Theotokos: Gecitkale Rd; Open 9am–5pm daily; Adm*

Royal Tombs
These Bronze Age graves have revealed gold, ivory and bronze objects that were meant to accompany kings into the after-life. Most are now in the Cyprus Museum (see pp10–11) but replicas are on-site. ✎ *Map J3 • Open Jun–Oct: 9am–7pm daily; Nov–May: 9am–1pm, 2–4:45pm daily • Adm*

Enkomi-Alasia
The best-preserved Bronze Age settlement on the island. ✎ *Map J3 • Open Jun–Oct: 9am–2pm daily; Nov–May: 9am–1pm, 2–4:45pm daily • Adm*

Iskele is also known as Trikomo

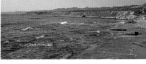

Left **"Acapulco Beach"** Right **Lara**

ⁱ⁰10 Northern Beaches

"Acapulco Beach"
This beautiful beach is the North's most popular stretch of sand and on summer weekends you certainly won't be alone – Turkish Cypriots from Nicosia flock here to escape the scorching heat of the city. Facilities include more hotels, watersports and restaurants than most of the region's beaches. 🚫 *Map F2*

Lara
Jagged rocks frame Lara's immaculate stretch of sand, which is usually much less busy than Acapulco. It has a couple of bar-restaurants serving snacks and cold drinks. 🚫 *Map F2*

Alagadi Halk Plaji
Endangered loggerhead and green turtles lay their eggs on this undeveloped crescent of sand and shingle. The Society for Protection of Turtles (SPOT) operates a small information centre and takes visitors on turtle-watching walks from May to October, during the nesting season, as well as doing its best to protect eggs and hatchlings. 🚫 *Map G2*

Onüçüncü Mil
This stretch of coast offers an arc of almost deserted, fine sand, backed by grassy dunes and pine trees and with craggy limestone headlands. One of the North's best options, close to Kyrenia. 🚫 *Map G2*

Salamis
Visitors to Salamis *(see p106)* can combine sightseeing with sunbathing at the long beach next to the ancient site. A reef protects shallow, clear water – good for snorkelling. 🚫 *Map J3*

Karaoglanoglou
In recent years Karaoglanoglou has blossomed into the North's main resort beach. Plenty of hotels, restaurants, bars and watersports. 🚫 *Map E2*

Paloura
A couple of basic snack bars and one (as yet uncompleted) hotel complement Paloura's clear blue water. 🚫 *Map K2*

Skoutari
There is super snorkelling around tiny Kilas Island, not far offshore from this long stretch of sand and pebbles midway along the Karpas Peninsula's south coast. 🚫 *Map L2*

Ronnas
A large, empty beach on the northern shore of the Karpas Peninsula, overlooked by pine woods. It is another nesting place for endangered green turtles. 🚫 *Map L1*

Nankomi
"Golden Beach" lives up to its nickname – a south-facing, uncrowded sweep of golden sand backed by rolling dunes. 🚫 *Map M1*

Left **Güzelyurt oranges** Right **Bellapais Abbey**

Northern Festivals

International Spring Concerts, Bellapais
The cloisters of Bellapais Abbey come alive every year during this season of classical concerts, which attract musicians and music-lovers from all over the world. ◈ May

Güzelyurt (Morphou) Orange Festival
Since 1977 Güzelyurt (Morphou) in Northern Cyprus's citrus-growing region has been the venue for a festival that originally celebrated the orange harvest. It has now expanded to include concerts, competitions and art exhibitions. ◈ May

North Cyprus International Music Festival, Bellapais
Bellapais is once again the stunning venue for this annual event, with performances by world-famous artistes. ◈ May–Jun

Gazimagusa (Famagusta) Music Festival
Claiming to be the best music event in the Mediterranean, the festival hosts world music ensembles and folk musicians from all five continents. ◈ Jun–Jul

Nicosia Festival of Drama
Open-air performances and events in historic venues are the keynote of Northern Nicosia's annual festival of theatre and dance. ◈ Dates vary

Kyrenia Olive Festival
Costumed dancers, traditional musicians, and lots of eating and drinking help celebrate the olive harvest. Most events are held in and around the floodlit Kyrenia Castle *(see p108)*. ◈ Dates vary

Mehmetcik Grape Festival
In the heart of northern Cyprus's vine-growing region, the village of Mehmetcik marks each successful wine-producing season with music, dancing and, of course, wine. ◈ Dates vary

Iskele (Trikomo) Traditional Festival
Village costumes and traditional Turkish musical instruments are brought out to celebrate one of Northern Cyprus's most venerable feasts. ◈ Dates vary

Lapta (Lapithos) Lemon Festival
The lemon-growing village of Lapta (Lapithos) throws a lively annual party in honour of the yellow citrus fruit that has long been emblematic of Cyprus. ◈ Dates vary

Seker Bayrami (Sugar Festival)
Feasts and family reunions mark the end of the Muslim religion's annual Ramadan fast. At this time everyone dons new clothes and makes up for a month of abstinence. ◈ Dates vary according to lunar calendar

The official currency in Northern Cyprus is the Turkish lira (YTL) but the euro is accepted and indicated in the price ranges.

Price Categories

For a three-course
meal for one with half | € | €10–€15
a bottle of wine (or | €€ | €15–€25
equivalent meal), taxes | €€€ | €25–€35
and extra charges. | €€€€ | €35–€50
| €€€€€ | over €50

Above **Canli Balik**

🔟 Places to Eat

Sez-i Fish Restaurant, Kyrenia

In the heart of Kyrenia's beach resort area, Sez-i is rated one of the best fish restaurants in Northern Cyprus – which is praise indeed. ✪ *Kervansaray, Karaoglanoglou • Map F2 • 822 30 60 • €€€€*

Mirabella, Kyrenia

This French-influenced restaurant on the outskirts of Kyrenia is a fitting place to spoil yourself on the last night of your holiday. ✪ *Karakum Rd • Map F2 • 815 73 90 • €€€*

Niazi's, Kyrenia

A local favourite, Niazi's (opposite the Dome Hotel) is highly regarded for its grills, kebabs and sticky desserts, and has a better than average wine list. ✪ *Kordonboyu • Map F2 • 815 21 60 • €€€€*

The Grapevine Bar and Restaurant, Kyrenia

An amiable British-influenced spot with a pubby atmosphere, the Grapevine is one of Kyrenia's social hubs and has a more imaginative menu than most local restaurants. ✪ *Ecevit Caddesi • Map F2 • 815 24 96 • €€€*

Canli Balik, Kyrenia

Friendly, busy harbour-side café with some tables under umbrellas on the quay, others on the terrace. Grilled fish and meze. ✪ *Kyrenia Harbour 104 • Map F2 • 815 21 82 • Dis. access • €€€*

Boghjalian Konak Restaurant, Nicosia

The only restaurant in the still being restored Arabahmet district serves lavish *meze* in an old courtyard, a private dining room, or an Ottoman-style banquet room upstairs. ✪ *Salahi Sevket Sok, Arabahmet • Map N2 • 228 07 00 • €€€*

Café Sedir, Nicosia

With tables beneath white umbrellas in a calm, cloistered courtyard, this is the best place in the old town for a rest and cold drink. ✪ *Büyük Han • Map P2 • No phone • Dis. access • €*

Avcilar, Nicosia

Favoured by Northern Cyprus's movers and shakers, Avcilar favours game and other hearty traditional dishes. Prepare for a feast. ✪ *Atatürk 130 • Map P1 • No phone • €€€*

Koca Reis Beach Bar, Salamis

Koca Reis is the best of a scattering of simple taverns along Salamis bay, serving fresh fish, salads and drinks. ✪ *Salamis beach • Map J3 • 378 82 29 • €€*

Desdemona Kebab and Meze House, Famagusta

Cheap and plentiful *meze* and kebabs are the mainstays of this eating-place, in a vault within the ramparts – a good place to escape the midday sun. ✪ *Canbulat Yolu • Map J4 • No phone • Dis. access • €€*

 Note: Unless otherwise stated, all restaurants accept credit cards and serve vegetarian meals

STREETSMART

CYPRUS'S TOP 10

Left **Agia Napa beach** Centre **Information booth** Right **Tourist office**

General Information

When to Go
Cyprus is a year-round destination. Temperatures on the coast rarely fall much below 15°C (59°F) even in winter, although snow often falls on the Troodos Mountains. December to February are the coolest, wettest months, and July and August the hottest, with temperatures rising as high as 40°C (104°F).

Passports & Visas, Southern Cyprus
Most visitors, including citizens of the EU, the USA, Canada, Australia and New Zealand, do not require a visa to visit the Republic of Cyprus and can stay for up to three months. However visitors will be refused entry if their passports show that they have entered via Northern Cyprus.

Passports & Visas, Northern Cyprus
Again, most visitors, including citizens of the EU, USA, Canada, Australia and New Zealand require only a valid passport to visit Northern Cyprus, but to avoid being refused entry on later visits to the south, passports should be stamped on a separate loose sheet of paper.

Tourist Offices
The Cyprus Tourism Organization (CTO), representing southern Cyprus, has overseas offices in the UK, USA, Germany,
Australia and elsewhere – see the website www.visitcyprus.org.cy for addresses. The North Cyprus Tourism Centre has overseas offices in the UK, Germany and Sweden – see the website www.go-northcyprus.com

Tourist Offices in Cyprus
The CTO has several outlets in southern Cyprus where you can access brochures, maps and information about the island. ✆ *Aristokyprou 11, Laiki Geitonia, Nicosia; 22 67 42 64 • Spyrou Araouzou 130, Limassol; 25 36 27 56 • Plateia Vasileos Pavlou, Larnaca; 24 65 43 22 • Gladstonos 3, Pafos; 26 93 28 41 • Leoforos Kryou Nerou 12, Agia Napa; 23 72 17 96*

Embassies and Consulates
Many countries have embassies or consulates in southern Nicosia *(see box)*, but there are none north of the "Green Line".

Customs
Visitors may bring in 200 cigarettes; one litre of spirits; two litres of wine; and 60 millilitres of perfume. The import of perishable food items is strictly prohibited.

Currency
Visitors may import any amount of Cypriot or foreign banknotes, which should be declared to
customs on arrival. There are no restrictions in the North, which has no currency of its own and uses the Turkish lira.

Weddings
Cyprus is one of the world's most popular wedding destinations and some hotels have their own wedding chapel. Bride and groom must stay in Cyprus for 20 days. ✆ *www.ucm.org.cy*

What to Take
Visitors taking medication should travel with an adequate supply. Pack beachwear and smart-casual wear for resorts, and a light sweater for spring and autumn visits. Remember your sun screen too.

Left **Passenger ferry** Right **Turkish Airlines plane**

ᵀᴼᴾ10 Getting to Cyprus

Package Holidays

Most visitors travel to Cyprus on a package holiday which combines flights, accommodation, transport to and from the airport, and, often, car hire, and can be the most cost-effective option. Specialist walking, diving, watersports and wedding packages are also available and lists of these and other holiday companies are available from CTO offices overseas (see p114).

By Scheduled Flight

The national flag carrier Cyprus Airways and numerous European airlines fly frequently to Larnaka and Pafos airports from many European capital cities. Scheduled flights can be more expensive than weekly charter flights, but offer more flexibility and greater comfort.

By Charter Flight

Many charter airlines fly to Pafos and Larnaka from European capital cities and regional hubs, with weekly departures. Some fly all year round, but the majority operate only from April to October. Most seats are sold as part of inclusive package holidays, but "flight only" charters are also available and can be affordable and convenient for holidaymakers who live far away from capital city airports.

By Ferry

Determined budget travellers can sail into Limassol from Piraeus (the port of Athens) and from the Greek islands of Patmos or Rhodes. They can also then travel on to Haifa in Israel, Port Said in Egypt or Beirut in Lebanon.

By Yacht

Although Cyprus is not on most yacht-sailor's Eastern Mediterranean itinerary, it is an ideal port of call on a longer yacht cruise from Rhodes in Greece and along the "Turquoise Coast" of Turkey, as the south of the island has some excellent marinas. Yachts must not land in Northern Cyprus before visiting the south.

By Cruise Ship

Cyprus is the cruising gateway to the Eastern Mediterranean and the Middle East, and a Cyprus holiday can be combined with a cruise to various destinations in Egypt, Israel and Lebanon.

Package Holidays, Northern Cyprus

The easiest way to visit Northern Cyprus is on a package holiday which offers the same combination of flights, accommodation, airport transport and, generally, car hire as those to the south. Lists of specialist tour operators offering package holidays are available from all the Northern Cyprus Tourist Centres overseas.

Northern Cyprus by Scheduled Flight

Cyprus Turkish Airlines and Turkish Airlines connect Northern Cyprus with Istanbul, Ankara and other Turkish cities. All scheduled flights to Ercan, the North's only airport, are via Turkey. It is not possible to fly direct to the North from any other country.

Northern Cyprus by Charter Flight

Most charter flights to the North are intended to be sold as part of a holiday package, but some "flight-only" deals are available and are the best bet for budget travellers. As with scheduled flights, all charter flights to the North must first land in Turkey.

Northern Cyprus by Ferry

Budget travellers who want to combine a visit to Northern Cyprus with a tour of mainland Turkey can catch the slow overnight ferry from Mersin in Turkey to Famagusta (operated by Turkish line TML) or make the faster catamaran crossing from Tasucu to Kyrenia, taking about three hours. Contact the North Cyprus Tourism Centre (see p114) for ferry schedules.

Left **Motorcycles for hire** Right **Taxi**

Getting Around Cyprus

1 By Car
Driving is the easiest way to get around southern Cyprus. Roads are generally good, with motorways connecting Nicosia with Larnaka, Limassol, Pafos and Agia Napa. Distances are short – it is less than 160 km (100 miles) from Pafos to Nicosia.

2 Car Hire
Car hire companies have offices in all four major towns in the south (Nicosia, Larnaka, Limassol and Pafos) and at Larnaka and Pafos airports. A full national or international driving licence is required, and drivers under 25 may require additional insurance cover. Rental cars may not be taken from the south into Northern Cyprus.

3 Rules of the Road
Cypriots drive on the left and road signs are in English as well as Greek in the south. Distances and speed limits are in kilometres – 100 kmph (60 mph) on motorways, 80 kmph (50 mph) on most other roads and 50 kmph (30 mph) unless otherwise indicated in built-up areas. There are on the spot fines for speeding and for failing to wear seatbelts. Drink-driving (more than 39 micrograms per 100ml) is a criminal offence, as is using a mobile phone while driving.

4 By Bus
There are at least six bus services daily between the four main southern towns. Local buses also connect outlying communities with the nearest main town, but they are geared to the needs of schoolchildren and villagers so departures are only early morning and mid-afternoon.

5 By Taxi
Metered taxis operate in all the main towns. Unmetered rural taxis serve most larger villages, charging 35–42 cents per kilometre. Shared "service taxis", which take passengers door to door, operate half-hourly between 6am and 6pm (7pm summer) Monday to Friday, and 7am to 5pm at weekends between all the major towns. Telephone to order a ride. ◈ *Service taxis:*
- *Nicosia: 22 73 08 88*
- *Limassol: 25 87 76 66*
- *Larnaca: 24 66 10 10*
- *Pafos: 26 93 31 81*
- *Islandwide: 77 77 74 74*

6 By Speedboat
Find out-of-the-way beaches and explore the wilder shores of the south of the island with a "self-drive" speedboat, hired by the day at Pafos and some other resorts. This is a great way to see the remote, uncrowded Akamas Peninsula in particular *(see pp 26–7)*.

7 By Bicycle
Bicycles can be hired by the day or week in Agia Napa, and are ideal for commuting to the beach. For more energetic cyclists, several specialist holiday companies offer escorted mountain-bike tours of the Troodos Mountains and other wilder, remoter parts of Cyprus. Details are available from the Cyprus Tourism Organization *(see p114)*.

8 By Motorcycle
Motorcycles, mopeds and scooters can be rented at all resorts and are a fun way to get around. A national or international motorcycle licence is required.

9 By Taxi, Northern Cyprus
Metered taxis operate in main towns and unmetered taxis operate to rural villages; for both, agree a fare before setting off. Shared taxis also operate between main towns at set fares, but tend to leave when full rather than operating to a schedule.

10 By Car, Northern Cyprus
Car rental is available in the North but the main international rental companies are absent and vehicle maintenance standards may be patchy. Make sure you have adequate insurance to cover all risks.

Left **Umbrella sun protection** Right **UN forces**

⁑10 Things to Avoid

Illegal Border Crossing

Do not attempt to cross the "Green Line" at any but the official crossing points. In Nicosia the Ledra Palace crossing is for pedestrians and the Agios Dometios for those in vehicles. In the Larnaka district the vehicle crossing is at Pergamos and in the Famagusta district at Strovilia. Crossing the line anywhere else is dangerous and may result in arrest *(see p65)*.

Military Zones

Britain's sovereign bases in the south, at Akrotiri (Episkopi) and Deryneia, are also used by US forces and are likely to be on heightened alert in these security-conscious times. Do not intrude on military installations. The same applies to Turkish Army personnel, equipment and installations in the occupied North.

Photography Restrictions

As well as avoiding taking photographs of military installations, vehicles and army personnel (including UN soldiers on the "Green Line"), it is best not to take photographs at airports or government buildings, especially in the North.

Sunburn

Cyprus has some of the hottest weather in Europe, and it is easy to get sunburnt any time from early April until late October. Young children are especially vulnerable. Sunhats, a high-factor sunscreen and sunblock are essential.

Mosquitoes

Although mosquitoes in Cyprus do not carry disease they can be a pest in summer. Most hotel rooms do not have plug-in deterrent dispensers, but these can be bought in all local stores. Repellent containing "deet" or citronella oil keeps them at bay outdoors after dark, but wear long sleeves and long trousers to reduce the risk of being bitten.

Cabarets and Clip Joints

Cyprus has its share of sleaze, with so-called "cabarets" featuring topless pole-dancers in Larnaka, Nicosia, Agia Napa and, especially, Limassol. Drinks are over-priced (sometimes by several noughts added to the bill), the atmosphere can be intimidating and credit card fraud is not uncommon.

Discussing Politics

The events of 1974, when the island was divided between the Turkish and the Greek Cypriots, are still remembered with bitterness. In both the south and the North, local people vehemently argue the justice of their cause. Politics and recent history are subjects that are best avoided.

"International" Restaurants

The Cypriot take on "international" cuisine is not always entirely successful. However much you may be craving your home cuisine, it is advisable to avoid restaurants that seem to try too hard to cater to every possible taste – and make too much use of the microwave oven. Local restaurants are always a better bet.

Drugs

In the 1990s Agia Napa's rise to fame as a clubbers' paradise prompted fears of increased drug use by the party crowd, and a crack-down by Cypriot police. Penalties for possession of any type of drugs are severe and Cypriot club owners are encouraged to turn in people seen using.

Late-Night Noise

Cyprus is keen to keep its image squeaky clean and efforts have been made to turn down the volume at clubs late at night (and early morning) in Agia Napa. However, those seeking peace and quiet may well prefer one of the less party-oriented resorts.

Left **Woodland camp site** Right **Picnic area**

🔟 Budget Tips

1 Travelling Off-Season

Visiting Cyprus off-season will ensure you get the best package holiday deals. In particular, avoid Christmas, Easter, British school holidays (late June to early September), and the Greek Orthodox Easter season (dates vary annually), when accommodation and flights are at a premium and prices soar.

2 Cheap Flights

Check with your local travel agent for "last-minute" flight-only charter deals: travellers who can be flexible about departure days, times and airports will inevitably get the best airfare deals.

3 Discounts

Students, school-children, teachers, academics and senior citizens are entitled to reduced admission fees at many museums, archaeological sites and other visitor attractions as long as they are able to show some proof of status. The Euro 26 Youth Card, available from the Cyprus Youth Board just outside Nicosia, entitles people aged 13 to 26 to a multitude of shopping, entertainment and transport discounts. 🔊 *Cyprus Youth Board: Anglantzia 62, Nicosia • Map F3 • 22 40 26 00 • info@youthboard. org.cy*

4 Self-Catering

Staying in a self-catering apartment *(see p128)* can have the benefit of providing big savings, especially for families. Buying food, wine, snacks and soft drinks at local shops and markets and preparing it yourselves is a way of getting considerably better value for money than eating at many of the tourist-orientated restaurants.

5 Hostels

Youth hostels are not just the preserve of the young and can offer very good value for those on a tight budget. However, don't expect to be offered any luxuries. 🔊 *Nicosia: Tefkrous; Map P3; 22 67 48 08 • Larnaka; Nicolaou Rossou 27; Map G5; 24 62 11 88*

6 Picnics

There are open-air markets selling fresh produce in all the main towns, and there are plenty of supermarkets and mini-markets to choose from in all the resorts. Putting together the ingredients for a picnic is not only easy but fun. It also offers a chance to mix with the locals and enjoy some delicious homegrown fare. There are picnic places, which have been designated by the Cyprus Tourism Organization, at many beaches and natural beauty spots.

7 Free Entertainment

Local tourist information offices at resorts can provide an up-to-date calendar of free events taking place nearby, ranging from village harvest festivals and religious processions to open-air concerts and cultural performances.

8 Camping

The following are campsites that are officially designated by the Cyprus Tourism Organization. 🔊 *Governor's Beach, Kalymnos; Map E6 25 63 28 78 • Geroskipou, 3km from Pafos centre; Map A5; 99 63 22 29 • Fengari, Coral Bay, 11km north of Pafos; Map A5; 26 62 15 34 • Polis: Map A4; 26 81 50 80*

9 Working Holidays

It is possible to find holiday work in Cyprus, especially in bars, clubs and restaurants, or, if you have the right qualifications, as a holiday rep. Hours are long, pay is generally low and working conditions less than perfect, but it can help to finance a longer stay.

10 Hitch-hiking

Hitching is permitted and Cypriots are quite generous in offering free rides. That said, waiting by the roadside in high summer is hot and thirsty work – wear a hat and take a water bottle.

Left **Cypriot bank** Right **Newspaper stand**

🔟 Banking and Communications

Currency
The official currency of the Republic of Cyprus is the euro (it replaced the Cypriot pound in January 2008), roughly equal to £0.79 in value. It is divided into 100 cents, and notes are in denominations of 5, 10, 20, 50, 100, 200 and 500. Northern Cyprus uses the Turkish lira (YTL), although the euro is accepted everywhere. If you wish to exchange Cypriot pound currency you may do so only at the Central Bank of Cyprus; notes can be changed until the end of 2017, and coins until the end of 2009.

Banks
Banks are open 8:15am–1pm Monday to Friday as well as 3:15–4:45pm on Mondays. Banks at Larnaka and Pafos airports stay open until the last night flight has arrived. Banks in the North open from 8am–noon Monday to Saturday.

ATMs
There are 24-hour automatic teller machines in the centre of all main resorts and towns in the south. ATMs are not available in the North.

Credit Cards
All major credit cards are widely accepted in the Republic of Cyprus. However, few establishments in Northern Cyprus accept credit cards.

Language
Greek is the official language in the south, although English is widely spoken, as is German. Both are less understood by Turkish Cypriots, although most workers in hotels and restaurants have some understanding.

Telephones
All public phones in the south can be used for international calls. Coin-operated phones accept 5, 10 and 20 cent coins. Phone cards are sold in banks, post offices, shops, kiosks and Cyprus Telecommunications Authority offices. Fewer public phones are available in the North and service is less reliable.

Post Offices
Main post offices in Nicosia, Larnaca, Pafos and Limassol are open Monday to Saturday, but generally only until 1:30pm on Wednesdays and Saturdays. Post offices in other areas are generally only open 7:30am–1:30pm Mondays to Fridays. Post offices in the North open 8am–1pm and 2–5pm Monday to Friday, and 8:30am–12:30pm on Saturdays. All mail from the North goes via Turkey.

Directory Enquiries

Directory Enquiries (South):
192

International Directory Enquiries (South):
194

Directory Enquiries (North):
118

International Operator (North):
115

Internet
Cyprus's efficient ISP CytaNet offers a "pay as you go" subscription-free connection costing around 0.059 cents per minute. For more information e-mail call.centre@cyta.cytanet.com.cy. There are Internet centres in all towns in southern Cyprus, but only a few in the North, where connection can be slower.

Newspapers and Magazines
British and European newspapers are available in resorts a day after publication. In the south the *Cyprus Mail* is published daily in English. The North also has an English-language newspaper, the heavily biased *Cyprus Times*.

TV and Radio
Channel 2 broadcasts the news and weather in English, while the BBC World Service and British Forces Broadcasting Service can be received in both south and North. Most resort hotels offer satellite TV channels.

Left **Pharmacy** Right **Fire engine**

ᴓ10 Security and Health

Emergency Numbers
In the south, English-speaking operators respond immediately to emergency calls. In the North there are separate phone numbers for each emergency service.

Police
Cyprus is a relatively safe island, providing you follow any border or military procedures *(see p117)*, but any crime should be reported to the police immediately.

Ambulance
For accidents or illness that require emergency treatment, Cyprus has an English-speaking ambulance service in both the south and the North.

Fire
There are two fire services in Cyprus – one covering general emergencies, the other dealing with forest fires that can break out in summer in the mountains. Dispose of anything flammable with due care.

Emergency Numbers

Southern Cyprus
Police, Ambulance, Fire: 112 or 199
Forest Fire: 1407

Northern Cyprus
Police: 155
Ambulance: 112
Fire: 199
Forest Fire: 177

Health Insurance
Cyprus is free from most dangerous infectious diseases (although AIDS is present) and no immunizations are required. Drinking tap water is safe. However all medical treatment must be paid for and comprehensive travel insurance to cover any hospital and medical charges, as well as emergency repatriation, is advisable.

Hospitals
All government-run General Hospitals have accident and emergency departments. ⊙ *Nicosia General Hospital: 22 60 30 00 • Limassol General Hospital: 25 80 11 00/25 30 57 70 • Larnaka General Hospital: 24 80 05 00/24 80 03 69 • Pafos General Hospital: 26 80 31 00 • Polis Hospital: 26 82 18 00*

Dental Care
There are private dentists in all major towns and resorts and most hotels can recommend a local practitioner. Dentists' fees must be paid immediately, and all dentists will provide a receipt for insurance purposes.

Pharmacies
Listings of local pharmacies can be found in the English-language *Cyprus Mail* or by dialling 192. These sell a full range of medicines and remedies. Pharmacists can also usually advise and provide remedies for minor ailments and injuries, but if you need specialist prescription drugs it is best to bring an adequate supply with you. All-night pharmacies can be contacted by dialling 192 or 11892, or leaving a recorded message on 90 90 14 12 (Nicosia); 90 90 14 15 (Limassol); 90 90 14 14 (Larnaka); 90 90 14 16 (Pafos); and 90 90 14 13 (Agia Napa).

Doctors
As with dentists, hotels can generally recommend a local doctor. Again, bills must be settled immediately, but doctors will provide a receipt for claiming back on insurance policies.

Crime
Both sectors of the island have fairly low crime rates. Tourists are rarely victims of violent crime, although there are occasional late-night scuffles between local youths and young male visitors. Valuables should be locked in the boot of hired cars and extra cash, credit cards, travellers' cheques and airline tickets should be kept in a hotel safe. Most larger hotels have in-room safes. Credit card fraud is on the increase so keep a record of all card transactions and check your bill on your return home.

Left **Wheelchair on a Cyprus beach** Right **Wheelchair ramp beside stairway**

Special Concerns

1 Sight and Hearing Disabilities

Sadly, few museums, archaeological sites or other attractions in the south (and none in the North) provide Braille or audio guides for visually impaired people, nor induction loop devices for those with hearing difficulties.

2 Wheelchair Access

Few public buildings, shops or visitor attractions have wheelchair ramps so access can be very difficult for wheelchair users. Many museums are in older buildings without lifts. Access to archaeological sites is also difficult. Pavements in towns and villages (if there are any) are often uneven. A leaflet giving limited information on facilities for wheelchair users is available from the CTO *(see p114)*.

3 Disability Organizations

The British charity RADAR (for people with hearing and visual impairment) can supply information on facilities in Cyprus and offer help for travellers with isabilities. ✎ *RADAR: www.radar.org.uk*

4 Travelling with Children

Main brands of baby food, medicines and toiletries such as nappies are sold in all supermarkets and pharmacies. Both parts of the island are family-friendly, with children welcomed everywhere and plenty of kids' facilities. However, risks for smaller children include sunburn, occasional rough waters on some beaches and pests such as jellyfish, sea urchins and stinging insects. Normal caution should be exercised.

5 Senior Citizens

Both Cypriot communities are notably respectful to older people, but hazards include urban traffic (Cypriot drivers sometimes ignore pedestrian crossings) and noise – Agia Napa, especially, is geared to younger visitors.

6 Women Travellers

Women travelling alone or together should exercise normal caution. Cyprus is generally safe, but there has been a rise in sexual assaults against women travellers so avoid walking alone at night.

7 Gay Travellers

Homosexuality is no longer illegal in southern Cyprus and gay visitors are generally tolerated; there are gay clubs and bars in Agia Napa, Larnaka, Limassol and Pafos and nude gay beaches at Kermia (near Agia Napa), Pissouri, Evdimou and "White Rocks" beach near Governor's Beach. However, there are occasional incidents of violence against gays. In Northern Cyprus homosexuality is still illegal.

8 Travelling with Pets

Animals, including dogs and cats, may not be brought into Northern or southern Cyprus.

9 Special Diets

People with special dietary needs, such as diabetes, lactose or gluten intolerance, or nut allergies, should seek detailed dietary advice before travelling and should treat many Cypriot dishes with caution. Groundnut oil is widely used in cooking and salad dressings in place of olive oil.

10 Single Travellers

Most visitors to Cyprus come as couples, families, or groups of singles, and most hotels offer only double or twin rooms and charge a "single supplement" for those travelling alone. Individuals travelling independently may be able to negotiate a better deal out of season. Several companies specialize in tours for singles: lists are available from the CTO *(see p114)* or the Association of Independent Tour Operators. ✎ *Association of Independent Tour Operators: www.aito.co.uk*

Left **Restaurant menu boards** Right **Snack bar**

Eating and Drinking Tips

Restaurants and Tavernas

Cyprus has more than its fair share of places to eat: as well as traditional tavernas, serving Greek and Turkish-influenced dishes, there are French, Italian, Mexican, Chinese, Thai, Indian, Middle Eastern, Russian and even Japanese restaurants. Fish is the most expensive item on the menu, although at coastal locales it is generally very fresh and tasty, so well worth the expense. Chicken is usually the cheapest meat dish available.

Cafés and Snack Bars

There are hundreds of cafés and snack bars selling Cypriot specialities such as *souvlaki (see p54)* and doner kebabs, as well as international favourites such as burgers, chips and pizza.

Fast Food

International fast food brands are making inroads into the south, and there are also plenty

Meze dishes

of ethnic restaurants that serve take-away meals. Most will deliver to apartments and villas, and even to hotels, although it is best to check whether the latter accept this practice.

Vegetarians

Cyprus has few dedicated vegetarian restaurants. Non-meat eaters may even be offered fish, chicken or vegetable dishes containing meat stock. However, many traditional *meze* dishes, such as humus, tahini, and other dips *(see p55)*, are tasty and meat-free, and there are plenty of fresh fruit and salad vegetables available.

Wine from the Barrel

Traditional tavernas often serve wine from the barrel *(apo to vareli)* in half-litre or one-litre carafes. It's usually cheaper than bottled wine, but quality is variable to say the least.

Local Beers and Spirits

Why pay a premium for imported beers and spirits when local brands north and south of the Green Line can be equally good? Aniseed flavoured *ouzo* and fiery *zivania* as well as *raki* are somewhat acquired tastes, but Cypriot brandy tastes just fine, especially in a brandy

sour, the island's favourite cocktail, made with fresh lemon juice, angostura bitters and club soda. Locally made vodka and gin are palatable too *(see p57)*.

Water

Local tap water is safe to drink, but too heavily chlorinated for some palates. Bottled mineral water from Troodos springs is available everywhere.

Soft Drinks

As well as familiar international soft drink brands, and cheaper, locally made versions, Cyprus offers a deliciously wide choice of freshly squeezed juices – orange, grapefruit, apple and pomegranate among them – as well as thirst-quenching freshly made lemonade.

Menus

Menus are almost always multilingual, but in smaller, simpler restaurants on the beach (especially in the North) or in less-visited mountain villages you may simply be invited into the kitchen to view what is available.

Service Charges

A 10 percent service charge is automatically added to all hotel and restaurant bills so tipping is optional. Taxi drivers and hotel porters also welcome a small tip.

Left **Luxury hotel pool** Right **Holiday villa**

Accommodation Tips

1 High and Low Seasons

Most hotels offer cheaper deals in low season (mid-November to mid-March) except for the Christmas period (20 December to 6 January). Rates are highest, and rooms hardest to find, from mid-June to mid-September.

2 Package Holidays

Booking a package holiday, with flights, coach transfers and accommodation all included in the price, is almost always cheaper than booking hotels and flights independently, although it offers less freedom on your holiday.

3 Reservations

Hotels in Cyprus can be reserved from abroad by telephone, fax, e-mail or on a growing number of accommodation websites. A deposit by credit card is normally required but may be refunded if the reservation is cancelled within an agreed period before the date of arrival.

4 Booking Before You Go

Booking a hotel room in advance is strongly advised. Most accommodation in Cyprus is contracted out one or more years in advance by large holiday companies and finding a comfortable room on arrival may be very difficult.

5 Booking on the Spot

If you do choose to arrive in Cyprus without pre-booked accommodation you can often find a room through the Cyprus Hotel Association's desks at Larnaka airport, or through tourist information offices at Larnaka and Pafos airports, Limassol harbour, and all major town centres. In the North, tourist agencies in Kyrenia can find hotel rooms for those arriving without a reservation.

6 Tipping

Tipping is welcome but optional in hotels in the North and the south, but if a porter or a maid has offered particularly good service, a small gratuity never goes amiss.

7 Hotel Grading

Hotels in southern Cyprus are graded from 1- to 5-stars by the Cyprus Tourism Organization. Hotels in Northern

Holiday apartment

Cyprus are also graded from 1- to 5-stars by the Turkish tourism ministry. In general, avoid establishments with less than 3 stars as they are likely to be slightly shabby and with few facilities.

8 Apartments

Holiday apartments in southern Cyprus are classified A, B or C by the Cyprus Tourism Organization. Most have a shared pool, a small, basic kitchen with cooker and fridge, and one to three bedrooms. Luxury apartments may have a full kitchen with dishwasher, maid service and linen service (see p128).

9 Villas

Villas usually have a private pool, parking space, garden or patio, and barbecue area as well as a fully equipped kitchen with washing machine and dishwasher, up to four bedrooms, and amenities such as stereos and satellite TV (see p127).

10 Village Houses

Stylishly restored houses and cottages, mostly in the attractive villages of the Troodos, offer character, charm and a taste of local life. Most have modern kitchens and bedrooms and lounges decorated with warm traditional fabrics and antiques. Some have a small garden or terrace.

Left **The Annabelle** Right **Louis Apolonia Beach**

🔟 Luxury Hotels

Anassa, Polis

Rated not just the best hotel in Cyprus but, according to some, the best in the Mediterranean, the Anassa oozes style. No expense has been spared in the decorating of this lavish property, set in landscaped grounds, above one of the finest beaches on the island and with views out to sea. The rooms are comfortable, and the staff attentive. ✪ *Map A4 • 26 32 29 00 • anassa@ thanoshotels.com. • Dis. access • €€€€€*

Elysium Beach Resort, Pafos

This colossal resort is only 2 km (1.5 miles) from Pafos harbour, but with four restaurants and three bars many residents feel no need to leave its confines. The 250 rooms include 23 split-level lofts, 12 studio suites, and 12 villas. Other facilities include a pool, gym, and a spa specializing in Ayurvedic treatments. ✪ *Vassilisis Verenikis • Map A5 • 26 84 44 44 • info@ elysium.com.cy • Dis. access • €€€€€*

The Annabelle, Pafos

Long regarded as Pafos's best hotel, it exudes quiet style, yet with all the fun and facilities of the town on your doorstep. ✪ *Poseidonis • Map A5 • 26 93 83 33 • the@ annabelle-hotel.com • Dis. access • €€€€€*

Pafos Amathus Beach Hotel, Pafos

This is a 5-star property, close to Pafos harbour, overlooking the sea and with attractive poolside gardens. ✪ *Poseidonis • Map A5 • 26 88 33 00 • pamathus@pamathus.com. cy • Dis. access • €€€€€*

Louis Apollonia Beach, Limassol

This fine hotel has a huge pool to complement its small private beach where there are watersports on offer. Rooms are spacious and well-equipped, and the restaurant overlooks the beach. ✪ *Georgiou 1, Germasogeia • Map D6 • 25 32 33 51 • apollonia@ louishotels.com • Dis. access • €€€€*

Louis Princess Beach, Larnaka

The Louis Princess stands on a huge stretch of uncrowded beach, but also has its own pool. Accommodation includes studios in two poolside wings, plus suites. There are two restaurants, three bars, a gym, sauna, and a children's activity centre. Larnaka's nightlife is only 10 minutes away. ✪ *Oroklini, Larnaka-Dekelia Rd • Map G5 • 24 64 55 00 • Dis. access • €€€€*

Golden Bay Beach Hotel, Larnaka

A miniature waterfall flows into the Golden Bay's turquoise pool, surrounded by manicured lawns and palm trees. The only 5-star hotel in Larnaka is right on the beach, with watersports galore, lavish rooms and fine dining. ✪ *Pila, Larnaka-Dekelia Rd • Map G5 • 24 64 54 44 • goldenbay@lordos.com.cy • Dis. access • €€€€*

Grecian Park Hotel, Protaras

Midway between Protaras and Agia Napa, the 5-star Grecian Park is gloriously isolated but also within easy reach of both resorts. There are superb views and the rooms are very comfortable. ✪ *Cape Greco • Map J4 • 23 84 40 00 • info@grecianpark.com • Dis. access • €€€€*

Holiday Inn Nicosia City Centre

The Holiday Inn is the best hotel within the ramparts of old Nicosia. The rooms are comfortable, and there's an indoor pool, three restaurants and a rooftop bar. ✪ *Regaena 70 • Map N2 • 22 71 27 12 • hinnicres@ cytanet.com.cy • €€€€*

Hilton Cyprus, Nicosia

Well located and elegant, the Hilton is the only 5-star hotel in Nicosia. It provides a variety of top-quality indoor and outdoor dining. ✪ *Archbishop Makarios III Ave • Map F3 • 22 37 77 77 • hiltoncyprus@hilton.com. cy • Dis. access • €€€€€*

Price Categories

For a standard, double room per night (with breakfast if included), taxes and extra charges.

€	under €50
€€	€50–€100
€€€	€100–€200
€€€€	€200–€300
€€€€€	over €300

Above **Hotel Riu Cypria Maris**

🏆10 Family-Friendly Resorts

Louis King Jason, Pafos

This resort complex is just 20 minutes from the centre of Pafos. There are three pools, including a children's pool, and the 78 rooms, laid out around well-kept gardens, all have satellite TV and a kitchenette. ◊ *Map A5* • 26 94 77 50 • kingjason@ louishotels.com • *Dis. access* • €€€€

Aeneas Hotel, Agia Napa

With its huge pool, this is the epitome of family-friendly luxury, on Agia Napa's favourite beach. There is a mini-club for children. ◊ *Nissi Beach* • *Map J4* • 23 72 40 00 • aeneas@aeneas.com.cy • *Dis. access* • €€€€

Malama Holiday Village, Agia Napa

The one- and two-bedroom suites at the Malama all have patios or verandahs, fully equipped kitchens and satellite TV. For kids, there's a playground with a bouncy castle, a pool, tennis, and the Malamino Kids Club offering parties, mini-discos, beach games and excursions. ◊ *Paralimni* • *Map J4* • 23 82 20 00 • info@malamaholidayvillage. com • *Dis. access* • €€€€

Olympic Lagoon Resort, Agia Napa

Three pools and a range of facilities, including mini-golf, floodlit tennis courts, pool tables and a

children's play area, make this one of the best choices in Agia Napa. ◊ *Map J4* • 23 72 25 00 • olympic@kanikahotels. com • *Dis. access* • €€€

Kanika Pantheon Hotel, Limassol

Minutes from the beach, the Kanika combines a full array of services and facilities for adults with child-friendly facilities including a children's pool. The 147 rooms all have sea views and private balcony. ◊ *Kanika Enaerios Complex* • *Map D6* • 25 59 11 11 • kanikap@cytanet.com.cy • *Dis. access* • €€€

Ermitage Beach Hotel, Limassol

The Ermitage has its own sandy beach with a choice of watersports. Accommodation is in self-catering apartments with one or two bedrooms, and there is a children's pool. ◊ *Map D6* • 25 32 32 30 • www.theermitage.com • *Dis. access* • €€€

Luca-Cypria Poseidonia Beach Hotel, Limassol

Surrounded by land-scaped gardens and with its own stretch of beach, the Poseidonia offers a children's playground and pool, a big choice of restaurants and bars, watersports and its own nightclub. ◊ *Map D6* • 25 32 10 00 • poseidonia@ dhcyprotels.com • *Dis. access* • €€€

Hotel Riu Cypria Maris, Geroskipou

This comfortable 4-star hotel stands on its own semi-private beach, with a huge pool (and a smaller toddlers' pool) and offers good value for money, with plenty of watersports and entertainment. ◊ *Poseidonis* • *Map A5* • 26 96 41 11 • cypriamaris@ dhcyprotels.com • *Dis. access* • €€€

Louis Agios Elias Village, Protaras

Overlooking Fig Tree Bay is this delightful village-style resort with accommodation in 140 cottages in landscaped grounds, surrounding a central square with supermarket, two restaurants and a kindergarten. The "Family World Centre" offers donkey rides, a pet farm, cinema and dancing lessons, and there's a programme of entertainment. ◊ *Map J4* • 23 83 13 00 • *Dis. access* • €€€

Columbia Beach Hotel, Pissouri

Located on a "Blue Flag" beach, the Columbia has a children's playground and pool, and offers baby-sitting services. There are also water sports and a tennis court. It is next door to the larger resort hotel under the same management (see p128). ◊ *Map C6* • 25 83 33 33 • columbia@ columbia-hotels.com • *Dis. access* • €€€

 Note: *Unless otherwise stated, all hotels accept credit cards, and have en-suite bathrooms and air conditioning*

Left **Louis Phaethon Beach** Right Iberostar Ledra Beach

TOP 10 All-Inclusive and Activity Resorts

1 Louis Phaethon Beach, Pafos

The huge, 4-star Louis Phaethon Beach offers all-inclusive rates and facilities that include two restaurants, three bars and three pools (one for kids). Also in the package are all non-motorized watersports, a sauna, Jacuzzi, squash and badminton, as well as meals. ◉ *Map A5 • 26 96 46 00 • phaethon@louishotels. com • Dis. access • €€€€*

2 Iberostar Ledra Beach, Pafos

This 4-star resort has comfortable rooms and a range of all-inclusive facilities, including adults' and children's pools, playground, three bars and a restaurant. A five-minute drive from Pafos, it is on one of the area's best beaches. ◉ *Map A5 • 26 96 48 48 • inforesv@ louishotels.com • Dis. access • €€€€*

3 St George's Hotel and Golf Resort, Pafos

One of the island's most elegant resorts, the St George's offers sports facilities ranging from squash courts, floodlit tennis courts, snooker tables and golf. Sharing these facilities is the St George's Gardens apart-ment hotel, with its own bar and restaurant and an amphitheatre. ◉ *Chlorakas • Map A5 • 26 84 50 00 • stgeorge@stgeorge-hotel. com • Dis. access • €€€€*

4 Alexander the Great Beach Hotel, Pafos

Choose from standard rooms or luxury suites at this superb resort over-looking Pafos harbour. Activities include tennis, volleyball and watersports, and eating places include a gourmet restaurant. ◉ *Poseidonis • Map A5 • 26 96 50 00 • alexander1@ kanikahotels.com.cy • Dis. access • €€€€*

5 Pafian Sun Holi-day Village, Pafos

Studios and apartments, all with satellite TV. The range of activities includes indoor and outdoor pools, gym and sauna, tennis and volleyball courts and a games room, as well as live entertainment. ◉ *8064 Pafos • Map A5 • 26 84 40 00 • secretary@ futurehotels.com.cy • Dis access • €€€*

6 Le Meridien Limassol Spa and Resort

This self-contained luxury resort has everything you could want: a shopping arcade, four tennis courts, basketball and badminton courts, sports bar, disco, Internet café, even a football pitch. The grounds are car-free – guests get around by bicycle or golf buggy. It also has a thalasso-therapy spa. ◉ *Amathous • Map D6 • 25 86 20 00 • sales@lemeridien cyprus.com • Dis. access • €€€€*

7 Miramare Bay Resort, Limassol

A state-of-the-art fitness club and spa, fully staffed by trained instructors, set this hotel apart. Thalasso-therapy is a speciality and there is an indoor sun-room pool for cooler days. ◉ *Amerikanas, Potamos Germasogeias • Map D6 • 25 88 81 00 • info@miramare.com.cy • Dis. access • €€€€*

8 Aktea Beach Tourist Village, Agia Napa

The largest and most up-market "tourist village" style accommodation in the Agia Napa region has indoor and outdoor pools, watersports, a gym, and is right on the beach. ◉ *Neofytou Poullou 10 • Map J4 • 23 84 50 00 • Dis. access • €€€*

9 Panthea Tourist Village, Agia Napa

This complex of apart-ments has indoor and out-door pools, live music and watersports. ◉ *Nissi Ave 19 • Map J4 • 23 72 42 00 • Dis. access • €€€*

10 Callisto, Agia Napa

The Callisto has a huge assortment of activities on offer, with indoor and outdoor swimming pools, a gym, tennis courts, and all the watersports you could wish for. ◉ *Leoforos Nissis • Map J4 • 23 72 45 00 • callisto@ aquasolhotels.com.cy • Dis. access • €€€*

Price Categories

For a double room per night (with breakfast if included), taxes and extra charges, or per night in a villa.

€ under €50
€€ €50–€100
€€€ €100–€200
€€€€ €200–€300
€€€€€ over €300

Above **Villa Eleni**

Villas

1 Elysium Royal Villas, Pafos

Each of the Elysium's 12 "Royal Villas" has its own landscaped garden and private pool. It is linked to the larger luxury resort of the same name (see p124) ◎ Vasilissis Venenikis • Map A5 • 26 84 44 44 • elysium@spidernet. com.cy • Dis. access • €€€€€

2 Villa Evi, Pafos

One of the few villas to have been awarded official deluxe status, Evi has three bedrooms and sleeps up to eight. Facilities include a pool. The bright lights of Pafos are not far away. ◎ Pegeia 8560 • Map A5 • 26 93 50 09 • €€€

3 Villa D'Amore, Pegeia

Between Pegeia village and Coral Bay, and less than 15 minutes drive from Pafos, Villa D'Amore overlooks the sea. The villa also has its own pool. ◎ Map A5 • 26 93 32 98 • info@villa-damore-cyprus.com • €€€

4 Villa Eleni, Pegeia

Set amid fields and vineyards, Villa Eleni is not far from Coral Bay and the quieter beaches of the Akamas peninsula (see pp26–7). An elegant modern two-storey building in Neo-Classical style, it has neatly kept lawns, a patio and a good-sized pool. ◎ Map A4 • €€€€

5 Cypria Aphrodite, Pegeia

This large and comfortable "home away from home" has better facilities than most villas, including the luxury of satellite TV, as well as air-conditioned bedrooms and, naturally, a pool. Coral Bay, the Akamas beaches and Pafos are all within easy reach. ◎ Pegeia 8560 • Map A4 • 26 96 44 00 • €€

6 Villa Aphrodite, Polis

This pretty lavender-painted villa is the nicest of a newly built "village" of self-contained holiday houses on the outskirts of Polis, right on the long beach. The two-storey houses are well-appointed, set around recently planted palms and flowering oleander. Each villa also benefits from its own pool. ◎ Olympian Beach Villas, Chrysochou, Polis • Map A4 • €€€

7 Bougainvillea, Polis

A choice of two villas, each sleeping six people and each with a pool, between unpretentious Polis and hideaway Neo Chorio. The beaches of Chrysochou Bay, the harbour tavernas of Lakki and the forested wilderness of the Akamas peninsula are not far away. ◎ Verginas 13 • Map A4 • 26 81 22 50 • €€€€

8 Chrysanthia, Neo Chorio

Chrysanthia is a larger-than-average family villa – it can sleep up to eight people in air-conditioned comfort, with its own pool and off-road parking, close to the sea and the harbour at Latsi. ◎ Neo Chorio 8852 • Map A4 • 24 63 36 73 • aretizan@ spidernet.com.cy • €€

9 Villa Michaella, Neo Chorio

Combining modern facilities with an old-fashioned welcome from the owners, Michaella is delightfully located overlooking Chrysochou Bay. It has a large pool and a beautifully kept garden, and sleeps up to six people. ◎ Neo Chorio 8852 • Map A4 • 26 32 12 24 • €€

10 Nausicaa Villa Suites, Protaras

Attached to the Louis Nausicaa Hotel at Fig Tree Bay (see p128), these offer the best of both worlds: the privacy and flexibility of a villa, with all the facilities of a luxury hotel on call. Each of the suites is self-contained with a fabulously appointed kitchen and dining room opening onto a private terrace, garden and pool with sea views. Upstairs are two double en-suite bedrooms. ◎ Sitarkas 17 • Map J4 • 23 83 11 60 • nausicaa@louishotels.com • Dis. access • €€€€

Note: Unless otherwise stated, all hotels accept credit cards, and have en-suite bathrooms and air conditioning

Left **Louis Nausicaa Beach** Right **Demetra Hotel Apartments**

Suites and Apartments

1 Louis Nausicaa Beach, Protaras

The best studios and apartments in southern Cyprus are to be found here, on a landscaped headland overlooking Fig Tree Bay. The low-rise complex of whitewashed buildings features two pools and a private beach. There's a small supermarket on site, but for those who do not choose to cater for themselves there is also a choice of bars and restaurants. ⓢ *Sitarkas 17 • Map J4 • 23 83 11 60 • nausicaa@louishotels.com • Dis. access • €€€€*

2 Columbia Beach Resort, Pissouri

More than 100 luxury suites, all built with recycled earthenware tiles in the style of a traditional village. All have their own kitchen and dining area, but the rate includes a buffet breakfast. Smaller suites, which sleep two to three people, can be connected to create family accommodation. ⓢ *Map C6 • 25 83 33 33 • columbia@columbia-hotels.com • Dis. access • €€€*

3 Daphne Hotel Apartments, Pafos

The Daphne, not far from Pafos harbour and very much in the centre of things, has a loyal following of guests who come back year after year. Affordable, friendly and well-managed, it has clean, bright one- and two-bed apartments and studios which overlook a sunny pool. ⓢ *Alkminis 3 • Map A5 • 26 93 35 00 • vestahol@logos.cy.net • €€*

4 Demetra Hotel Apartments, Pafos

This comfortable combination of hotel and self-catering complex in the centre of Pafos is well-kept and prettily decorated. It has a surprisingly grand restaurant on its ground floor, as well as a pleasant pavement café. ⓢ *Artemidos 4 • Map A5 • 26 93 44 44 • demetrahotel@ cytanet.com.cy • €€€*

5 Corallia Beach, Pafos

Overlooking Coral Bay, this complex of studios and one-bedroom apartments has a fine location and a good choice of facilities, including a restaurant, bar, pool and even room service. ⓢ *Coral Bay • Map A5 • 26 62 21 21 • corallia.beach@ cytanet.com.cy • €€€*

6 Lover's Nest Valley, Polis

The friendly Lover's Nest Valley has just 30 studios and one-bedroom apartments but a wider range of facilities than any of its local rivals, including a pool, a laundry, a bar (but no restaurant) and air conditioning. ⓢ *Vasileos Stassikou 17, 20 • Map A4 • 26 32 24 01 • €€*

7 Vias Apartments, Agia Napa

Best described as cheap and cheerful, this small apartment complex offers great value for money. There are 44 studios and apartments, built around a small pool but not far from one of the area's better beaches. ⓢ *Kriou Nerou • Map J4 • 23 72 23 00 • €€*

8 Kermia Beach, Agia Napa

The Kermia Beach is for those who like plenty of activity, along with the flexibility of a self-catering apartment. There are 154 of these on site, all with air conditioning, pay TV and telephone, plus restaurant, bar, mini-golf, tennis and other activities. ⓢ *Leoforos Cavo Greco 74 • Map J4 • 23 72 14 01 • welcome@ kermiabeach.com • €€€*

9 L'Onda Beach Apartments, Limassol

L'Onda has its own pool, and accommodation is in one- and two-bedroom apartments. ⓢ *Georgiou A, Germasogeias • Map D6 • 25 32 18 21 • info@ londabeach.com • €€*

10 Chrielka Hotel Suites, Limassol

This functional suite hotel, overlooking the Municipal Gardens, is handy for the town centre. ⓢ *Olympion 7 • Map D6 • 25 35 83 66 • chrielkasuites@cytanet. com.cy • €€€*

Above **Kinyras**

Price Categories

For a standard, double room per night (with breakfast if included), taxes and extra charges.	€ under €50
	€€ €50–€100
	€€€ €100–€200
	€€€€ €200–€300
	€€€€€ over €300

TOP 10 Traditional Guesthouses

Kinyras, Pafos
Just off Ktima Pafos's central square, Kinyras is a characterful old townhouse that has been turned into a stylish guesthouse. Paintings and sculptures by young artists from the Cyprus College of Art at nearby Lempa adorn the foyer, corridors and rooms. There's a courtyard café and a restaurant with a menu of the best traditional Cypriot cooking. ◈ Archiepiskopou Makariou 91 • Map A5 • 26 94 16 04 • info@kiniras.cy.net • €€

Kostaris, Pafos
These stone-built houses and adjoining cottage share a pretty garden in which there is a traditional clay oven, an old wine-press and – best of all – a small pool. All three houses are furnished with charm, and share fabulous views. ◈ 8850 Goudi • Map A5 • 99 62 66 72 • kostaris@ cytanet.com.cy • €

The Spanos House, Pafos
This lovely family home stands in the middle of an orange grove and has been renovated to provide all you could wish for – including a swimming pool among the trees, which is shared between the one-bedroom house and two self-contained studio apartments. ◈ 8850 Goudi • Map A5 • 26 94 48 33 • kostaris@ cytanet.com.cy • €

To Spiti tis Rigenas, Larnaka
Built in the mid-19th century by the prominent Rigenas family, this mellow family home has a stone-paved courtyard full of flowers, three double bedrooms, a pool, and is 9 km (5.5 miles) from the nearest beach. ◈ Grigori Afxentiou 38, Oroklini • Map G5 • 24 64 60 00 • agrotourismo@ cytanet.com.cy • €€€

Kontoyannis House, Kalavassos
This old village home in the centre of Kalavassos has been tastefully converted into four studios and apartments, which share a pretty courtyard. Nearby are the sandy coves of Governor's Beach (see p40). ◈ Map E5 • 25 58 03 05 • agrotourismo@cytanet. com.cy • €€€

Stratos House, Kalavassos
Stratos is only steps away from the village square, with a beautiful arcaded courtyard off which open two large studio rooms, each with their own en-suite bathroom and kitchenette. On the upper floor is a lovely vine-covered verandah. Sensitively renovated, the house still retains much of its original 19th-century character. ◈ Map E5 • 24 33 22 93 • agrotourismo@ cytanet.com.cy • €€€

Angela's Stone House, Tochni
In the centre of Tochni is this 19th-century stone house which has been lovingly restored. Two bedrooms, a balcony, and a courtyard filled with lemon trees and pomegranates. ◈ Map E5 • 24 33 25 41 • agrotourismo@ cytanet.com.cy • €€€

Socrates House, Tochni
Modern comforts such as air conditioning and in-room TV, all within a beautiful traditional building. An old olive mill stands in the courtyard, and the guesthouse's taverna serves traditional meals. ◈ Map E5 • 24 33 36 36 • agrotourismo@ cytanet.com.cy • €€

Danae House, Tochni
Standing high above Tochni is this traditionally designed complex of eight one-bedroomed cottages, each with a sitting room, verandah or balcony, as well as a shared pool. ◈ Map E5 • 24 66 21 23 • danae@ spidernet.com.cy • €€€

Vasilopoulos House, Tochni
One of the oldest houses in Tochni now contains three one-bedroom apartments and five studios, each with a kitchen and all opening onto a shady courtyard. ◈ Map E5 • 24 33 25 31 • info@vasilo pouloshouse.com.cy • €€

Note: Unless otherwise stated, all hotels accept credit cards, and have en-suite bathrooms and air conditioning

Left **Merit Crystal Cove Hotel** Right **The Colony**

Northern Cyprus Resorts

The Colony, Kyrenia

The grand façade of the most luxurious hotel in Northern Cyprus cannot fail to impress, and inside it lives up to first impressions, with a marble foyer, spacious rooms and attentive staff. A lovely pool terrace on the first floor looks out over the roofs of Kyrenia. Only 20 minutes away is the hotel's private beach, and a shuttle bus takes you there. ⊗ *Ecevit Caddesi • Map F2 • 0392 815 1518 • thecolony@ parkheritage.com • Dis. access • €€€€€*

Chateau Lambousa, Kyrenia

Regarded as one of the very best hotels in the North until the opening of The Colony in 2003. With its location on the beach, the Lambousa is still a fine hotel which has more than earned its reputation. ⊗ *Map F2 • 0392 821 8751 • chateaulambousa@ northcyprus.net • Dis. access • €€€€*

Kyrenia Jasmine Court Hotel

One of only a few hotels in Northern Cyprus to have been awarded 5-star classification, Jasmine Court has a beachside location, super views, and luxurious rooms and restaurants. ⊗ *Map F2 • 0392 815 1450 • info@ jasminecourthotel.com • Dis. access • €€€€*

Merit Crystal Cove Hotel, Kyrenia

Perched above the sea about 15 km (10 miles) west of Kyrenia, this huge modern hotel would not look out of place in Las Vegas. With landscaped grounds, two swimming pools, a private beach and one of the North's smartest casinos, it really feels like a tropical island hide-away. ⊗ *Map F2 • 0392 821 2345 • www.merit crystalcove.com • Dis. access • €€€€*

Denizkizi Royal Hotel, Kyrenia

Wooded grounds surround the air-conditioned suites here. There is an array of bars and restaurants, a huge swimming pool, fitness centre and a choice of watersports. ⊗ *230 Alsancak • Map F2 • 0392 821 2676 • info@denizkizi. com • €€€*

Riverside Holiday Village, Kyrenia

Accommodation here is in one-, two- or three-bedroom cottages or villas with self-catering facilities, but there are also several restaurants and bars if you don't want to cook for yourself. Facilities include swimming pools, tennis court, volleyball and horse-riding. ⊗ *Alsancak • Map F2 • 0392 821 8906 • riverside@riversideholiday village.com • €€€*

Kyrenia Oscar Resort

The Kyrenia Oscar Resort offers spacious rooms and suites, a pool and a location near one of the region's best beaches. ⊗ *Map F2 • 0392 815 4801 • info@oscar-resort.com.tr • €€€*

Yazade House, Kyrenia

This delightful assortment of studios, apartments and villas is owned by an English couple. There is a pool in the courtyard. ⊗ *Yazicizade Sokak • Map F2 • 0392 815 57 69 • kay@yazade-house.com • €€€*

Bilfer Palm Beach Hotel, Famagusta

Overlooking the sandy beach north of Famagusta, this medium-size hotel is comfortable and well-appointed despite its rather undistinguished 1970s-style architecture. Facilities include tennis courts, a gym, Turkish bath, pool, restaurant and terrace bar, as well as a casino and nightclub. ⊗ *Kemel Server Caddesi • Map J4 • 0392 366 2000 • palmbeach@bilferhotel. com • Dis. access • €€€*

Salamis Bay Conti Resort

At this huge hotel most rooms have sea views, and there is a large pool and an adjacent beach. ⊗ *Map J3 • 0392 378 8201 • info@salamisbayconti.com • Dis. access • €€€*

  Note: *Unless otherwise stated, all hotels accept credit cards, and have en-suite bathrooms and air conditioning*

Price Categories

For a standard, double room per night (with breakfast if included), taxes and extra charges.

€ under €50
€€ €50–€100
€€€ €100–€200
€€€€ €200–€300
€€€€€ over €300

Above **Dome Hotel**

🔟 Northern Cyprus Hotels

1 Dome Hotel, Kyrenia

During the British colonial era the Dome was the poshest hotel in Kyrenia and the summer and weekend haunt of wealthy British expats. Although it has now been eclipsed by lavish new competitors, it has a nostalgic style and, with its location close to Kyrenia's pretty harbour, is a handy base for exploring the region. ◈ Map F2 • 0392 815 2772 • www.domehotel.com • Dis. access • €€€

2 Liman Hotel Casino, Kyrenia

Overlooking the harbour, the Liman is a quietly stylish hotel that appears to make most of its profits from its small casino. Bow-tied doormen stand on duty day and night. The hotel's outdoor restaurant across the street is a very pleasant place enjoy breakfast. ◈ Map F2 • 0392 815 2001 • liman@northcyprus.net • €€€

3 Mare Monte Hotel, Kyrenia

The Mare Monte is a medium-sized hotel at Kyrenia's beachside suburb of Alsancak, with wooded grounds and striking views of the Mediterranean and the dramatic Kyrenia range. It has a small pool. ◈ Alsancak • Map F2 • 0392 821 8310 • marmonte@kttc.net • €€

4 King's Court Hotel, Kyrenia

This village-style resort hotel, set among lemon and orange groves about 8 km (5 miles) west of Kyrenia harbour, is remarkable value for money, with a large pool, bar and restaurant, all minutes from a sandy beach. ◈ 242 Alsancak • Map F2 • 0392 821 8495 • info@kings-hotel.com • Dis. access • €€

5 Pitoresk Holiday Village, Kyrenia

A bungalow resort spread out around a garden filled with singing birds. Accommodation is in self-catering duplexes or studio apartments and there's a large pool. ◈ Orhan Durusoy Caddesi • Map F2 • 0392 815 6222 • info@pitoresk-northcyprus.com • Dis. access • €€€

6 Hotel Sempati, Kyrenia

All the rooms in this comfortable 3-star hotel have sea views and balconies, and there is a choice of accommodation in the main wing or in self-catering bungalows around the pool. ◈ Ali Ocak Sokak 24, Lapta • Map F2 • 0392 821 2770 • hotelsempati@hotelsempati.com • €€

7 Bellapais Gardens, Bellapais

Close to the spectacular ruin of Bellapais Abbey (see p105), this atmospheric small hotel really rates higher than its 3-star classification. It has pretty gardens shaded by cypresses and palm trees, a good pool, and a well-deserved reputation for excellent Turkish Cypriot cooking. High above sea level, it also offers a cool refuge from the north coast's blazing heat. ◈ Crusader Rd • Map F3 • 0392 815 6066 • info@bellapaisgardens.com • €€

8 Portofino Hotel, Famagusta

Rooms are large here, and all have balconies. There is a pleasant rooftop pool and café-restaurant with views of the medieval town. ◈ Fevzi Çakmak Caddesi 9 • Map J4 • 0392 366 4392 • reservation@portofinohotel-cyprus.com • Dis. access • €€€

9 Lefke Gardens Hotel, Lefke

Rooms in this hotel are plain but comfortable, and there is a garden. ◈ Map C3 • 0392 728 8223 • lefkegardens@veezy.com • €€

10 City Royal Hotel Nicosia

The best value place to stay in town. Rooms have air conditioning and a minibar and there is an indoor pool, a Turkish bath and casino. ◈ 19 Kemal Aşik Caddesi • Map F3 • 0392 228 7621 • royalhotel@northcyprus.net • Dis. access • €€€

The official currency of Northern Cyprus is the Turkish Lira (YTL) but the euro is accepted and indicated above.

General Index

Index

Index

Acknowledgements

Main Contributor
Scottish-born author Jack Hughes first visited Cyprus in 1974 and has travelled widely around the island ever since. Educated at Edinburgh University, he now lives in London, and is the author of numerous guidebooks to destinations around the world.

Produced by Sargasso Media Ltd, London

Editorial Director
Zoë Ross

Art Editor
Janis Utton

Picture Research
Helen Stallion

Proofreader
Stewart J Wild

Editorial Assistance
John Vickers

Photographers
Robin Gauldie, Jon Spaull

Illustrator
chrisorr.com

FOR DORLING KINDERSLEY

Publisher
Douglas Amrine

Publishing Manager
Anna Streiffert

Managing Art Editor
Kate Poole

Senior Cartographic Editor
Casper Morris

DTP
Jason Little

Production
Bethan Blase

Maps
James Macdonald, Mapping Ideas Ltd

Design and Editorial Assistance
Rachel Barber, Anna Freiberger, Carole French, Juliet Kenny Marianne Petrou, Pete Quinlan, Ellen Root

Special Assistance
The author would like to thank the following companies for their assistance while researching this book: Cyprus Tourism Organization; Direct Holidays; Louis Hotels; Small Luxury Hotels.

Picture Credits
t-top; tc-top centre; tr-top right; cla-centre left above; ca-centre above; cra-centre right above; cl-centre left; c-centre; cr-centre right; clb-centre left below; cb-centre below; crb-centre right below; bl-below left; bc-below centre; br-below right.

Every effort has been made to trace the copyright holders of images, and we apologize in advance for any unintentional omissions. We would be pleased to insert the appropriate acknowledgements in

Acknowledgements

any subsequent edition of this publication.

The publishers would like to thank the following individuals, companies, and picture libraries for permission to reproduce their photographs:

ALAMY IMAGES: Werner Otto 33tl; ANCIENT ART & ARCHITECTURE COLLECTION LTD: 10bl, 10br, 11t, 11cr, 11br, 32tr

CORBIS: 7tr, 7br, 28tl, 28tr, 28cra, 29tl, 29tr, 29tb, 30tr, 34tr, 42tr, 43tl, 44tr, 44b, 49cl, 60–61, 62tr, 72–3, 86–7, 90tr, 96tl, 100–01, 106tl, 108tl, 108tr, 110tl, 110tr, 115tl, 117tr; CYPRUS TOURISM ORGANIZATION: 46tr, 46br, 58tl, 58tr

SONIA HALLIDAY: 11bl, 22b, 22–3, 23t, 23b

IMAGES OF CYPRUS: 45bl, 47cl, 51r, 58bl, 59r

MUNICIPAL FOLK ART MUSEUM: 19bl; MUSEUM OF THE HISTORY OF CYPRIOT COINAGE/Vassos Stylianou: 33r

PETER JOUSIFFE: 104tr, 104cr, 105tr, 105b, 106cr, 107bl, 109tl; PICTURES COLOUR LIBRARY: Penelope Smythe 53tr; PIERIDES FOUNDATION MUSEUM: 14cl, 14b, 14–15, 15t, 15c, 15b

TIME OUT CYPRUS: 78tl, 92tr; TURKISH AIRLINES: 115tr

WORLD PICTURES: 46tl, 76tl, 97bl, 102tl, 112–13

All other images are © Dorling Kindersley. For further information see: www.dkimages.com

Special Editions of DK Travel Guides

DK Travel Guides can be purchased in bulk quantities at discounted prices for use in promotions or as premiums. We are also able to offer special editions and personalized jackets, corporate imprints, and excerpts from all of our books, tailored specifically to meet your own needs.

To find out more, please contact:

(in the United States) **SpecialSales@dk.com**

(in the UK) **Sarah.Burgess@dk.com**

(in Canada) DK Special Sales at **general@tourmaline.ca**

(in Australia) **business.development @pearson.com.au**

Phrase Book

In an Emergency

Help!	Voítheia!	vo-ee-theea!
Stop!	Stamatiste!	sta-ma-tee-steh!
Call an ambulance/ the police/ fire brigade!	Kaléste to asthenofóro/ tin astynomía/ tin pyrosvestiki	ka-le-steh to as-the-no-fo-ro/ teen a-sti-no-mía/teen pee-ro-zve-stee-kee!

Communication Essentials

Yes	Nai	neh
No	Ochi	o-chee
Please	Parakaló	pa-ra-ka-lo
Thank you	Efcharistó	ef-cha-ree-sto
You are welcome	Parakaló	pa-ra-ka-lo
OK/all right	Entáxei	en-dak-zee
Excuse me	Me synchoreite	me seen-cho-ree-teh
Hello	Geiá sas	yeea sas
Goodbye	Antio	an-dee-o
Good morning	Kaliméra	ka-lee-me-ra
Good night	Kalin'ychta	ka-lee-neech-ta
Here	Edó	ed-o
There	Ekei	e-kee
What?	Tí?	tee?
Why?	Giati?	ya-tee?
Where?	Poú?	poo?
Wait!	Perimene!	pe-ree-me-neh!
How do you do?	Pós eiste?	pos ees-te?
Pleased to meet you.	Chairo pol'y.	che-ro po-lee
Where is/are...?	Poú einai...?	poo ee-ne...?
How do I get to...?	Pós mporó na páo...?	pos bo-ro-na pa-o...?
Do you speak English?	Miláte Angliká?	mee-la-te an-glee-ka?
I don't understand.	Den katalavaino.	then ka-ta-la-ve-no.
I'm sorry.	Me synchoreite.	me seen-cho-ree teh.

Useful Words

big	Megálo	me-ga-lo
small	Mikró	mi-kro
hot	Zestó	zes-to
cold	Kr'yo	kree-o
good	Kaló	ka-lo
bad	Kakó	ka-ko
open	Anoichtá	a-neech-ta
closed	Kleistá	klee-sta
left	Aristerá	a-ree-ste-ra
right	Dexiá	dek-see-a
entrance	I eisodos	ee ee-so-thos
exit	I éxodos	ee e-kso-dos
toilet	Oi toualétes /	ee-too-a-le-tes
free/no charge	Doreán	tho-re-an

Shopping

How much does this cost?	Póso kánei?	po-so ka-nee?
I would like.....	Thelo...	the-lo...
Do you have...?	Echete...?	e-che-teh...?
What time do you open/close?	Póte anoigete/ kleinete?	po-teh a-nee-ye-teh/ klee-ne-teh?
This one.	Aftó edó.	af-to e-do.
That one.	Ekeino.	e-kee-no.
expensive	Akrivó	a-kree-vo
cheap	Fthinó	fthee-no
size	To mégethos	to me-ge-thos

Types of Shop

antiques shop	Magazi me antikes	ma-ga-zee me an-dee-kes
bakery	O foúrnos	o foor-nos
bank	I trápeza	ee tra-pe-za
bazaar	To pazári	to pa-za-ree
butcher	To kreopoleio	to kre-o-po-lee-o
cake shop	To zacharo-plasteio	to za-cha-ro-pla-stee-o
greengrocer	To manáviko	to ma-na-vee-ko
street market	I laïki agorá	ee la-ee-kee a-go-ra
newsagent	O efimeridopólis	O e-fee-me-ree-tho-po-lees
pharmacy	To farmakeio	to far-ma-kee-o
post office	To tachydromeio	to ta-chee-thro-mee-o
tobacconist	Eidi kapnistoú	Ee-thee kap-neesto
travel agent	To taxeidiotikó grafeio	to tak-see-thy-o-tee-ko gra-fee-o

Sightseeing

tourist information	O KOT	O KOT
archaeological	archaiologikós	ar-che-o-lo-yee kos
art gallery	I gkaleri	ee ga-le-ree
beach	I paralia	ee pa-ra-lee-a
castle	To kástro	to ka-stro

Greek is the official language of Cyprus, although Turkish is spoken in the occupied north of the island,. English is widely understood in the major resorts everywhere

cathedral	**O kathedrikos naos**	O kath-eth-rikos na-os
cave	**To spilaio**	to spee-le-o
church	**I ekklisía**	ee e-klee-see-a
monastery	**moní**	mo-ní
museum	**To mouseío**	to moo-see-o
park	**To párko**	to par-ko
river	**To potámi**	to po-ta-mee
road	**O drómos**	o thro-mos
town hall	**To dimarcheío**	to thee-mar-chee-o
closed on public holidays	**kleistó tis argíes**	klee-sto tees aryee-es

Transport

ticket office	**Ekdotíria eisitiríon**	ek-tho-tee-reea ee-see-tee-ree-on
return ticket	**Eisitírio me epistrofí**	ee-see-tee-ree-o meh e-pee-stro-fee
single journey	**Apló eisitírio**	a-pló ee-see-tee-reeo
bus station	**O stathmós leoforeíon**	o stath-mos leo-fo-ree-on
port	**To limán**	to lee-ma-nee
bicycle	**To podílato**	to po-thee-la-to
taxi	**To taxí**	to tak-see
airport	**To aerodrómio**	to a-e-ro-thro-mee-o

Staying in a Hotel

Do you have a vacant room?	**Echete domátia?**	e-che-teh tho-ma-tee-a?
I have a reservation.	**Echo kánei krátisi.**	e-cho ka-nee kra-tee-see.
double/twin room	**Díklino/me diplό kreváti**	thee-klee-no/ meh mo-na kre-vat-ya
single room	**Monóklino**	mo-no-klee-no
room with a bath/shower	**Domátio me mpánio/douz**	tho-ma-tee-o meh ban-yo/dooz

Eating Out

Have you got a table?	**Echete trapézi?**	e-che-te tra-pe-zee?
The bill	**Ton logariazmó**	ton lo-gar-yas-mo
waiter/waitress	**K'yrie/Kyría**	kee-ree-eh/ kee-ree-a
menu	**O katálogos**	o ka-ta-lo-gos
wine list	**O katálogos ton krasion**	o ka-ta-lo-gos ton krasion
breakfast	**To proïnó**	to pro-ee-no
lunch	**To mesimerianó**	to me-see-mer-ya-no

| dinner | **To deípno** | to theep-no |
| restaurant | **To estiatório** | to e-stee-a-to-ree-o |

Menu Decoder

aláti	a-la-tee	salt
angoúri	an-goo-ree	cucumber
baklavá	bak-la-vá	pastry with nuts and honey
bíra	bee-ra	beer
chaloúmi	cha-loo-mee	cow's milk cheese
chtapódi	chta-po-dee	octopus
domátes	dom-a-tes	tomatoes
eliés	el-ee-es	olives
fakés	fa-kes	lentils
fasólia	fas-o-lee-a	beans
fétta	fe-ta	goat's cheese
gála	ga-la	milk
hórta	hor-ta	vegetables
hoúmmos	hoo-moos	chickpea dip
kafés	ka-fes	coffee
me gála	me ga-la	with milk
skétos	ske-tos	black
glykýs	glee-kees	with sugar
chorís záchari	chor-rees za-cha-ree	without sugar
keftédhes	kef-ted-es	meatballs
khimos	kee-mos	fruit juice
kléftiko	klef-tee-ko	baked lamb
kotópoulo	kot-o-poo-lo	chicken
kounélli	koo-nel-ee	rabbit
krasí	kra-see	wine
áspro	as-pro	white
mávro	mav-ro	red
rosé	ro-ze	rosé
kremidhi	krem-ee-dee	onion
loukániko	loo-kan-ee-ko	sausage
loukoúmi	loo-koo-mee	Turkish delight
manitária	man-ee-taree-a	mushrooms
maroúli	mar-oo-lee	lettuce
melitzána	mel-eet-za-na	aubergine (eggplant)
midhya	mee-dee-ya	mussels
moussaká	moo-sa-ka	minced meat with aubergine (eggplant) in a white sauce
neró	ne-ro	water
oúzo	oo-zo	aniseed liqueur
pagotó	pa-go-to	ice cream
paidháki	payd-ha-kee	lamb chop
patátes	pa-ta-tes	potatoes
pikándikos	pee-kan-dee-kos	spicy

pipéri	pip-er-ree	pepper
pipérya	pip-er-ree-a	pepper (vegetable)
pitta	pee-ta	flat bread
portokáli	por-to-ka-lee	orange
psári	psa-ree	fish
psiménos	psee-me-nos	roasted
psitós	psee-tos	grilled
psomí	pso-mee	bread
saláta	sal-a-ta	salad
sardhéles	sard-hel-es	sardines
sheftália	shef-ta-lee-a	lamb sausage
skórdho	skord-ho	garlic
soúpa	soo-pa	soup
souvláki	soov-la-kee	grilled meat kebab
spanáhi	spa-na-hee	spinach
stafília	sta-fil-ee-a	grapes
stifádho	stif-a-do	beef in onion and tomato sauce
táhini	ta-hee-nee	sesame seed dip
taramás	ta-ra-mas	fish-roe dip
tighanitós	tee-gan-nee-tos	fried
tsái	tsa-ee	tea
tyrí	tee-ree	cheese
vodhinó kréas	vod-hee-no kree-as	beef
voútiro	voo-tee-ro	butter
vrazménos	vraz-me-nos	boiled
yaoúrti	ya-oor-tee	yoghurt
zambón	zam-bon	ham

Numbers

1	éna	e-na
2	d'yo	thee-o
3	tría	tree-a
4	téssera	te-se-ra
5	pénte	pen-deh
6	éxi	ek-si
7	eptá	ep-ta
8	ochtó	och-to
9	ennéa	e-ne-a
10	déka	the-ka
11	énteka	en-de-ka
12	dódeka	tho-the-ka
13	dekatría	de-ka-tree-a
14	dekatéssera	the-ka-tes-se-ra
15	dekapénte	the-ka-pen-de
16	dekaéxi	the-ka-ek-si
17	dekaeptá	the-ka-ep-ta
18	dekaochtó	the-ka-och-to
19	dekaennéa	the-ka-e-ne-a
20	eikosi	ee-ko-see
30	triánta	tree-an-da
40	saránta	sa-ran-da
50	peninta	pe-neen-da
60	exínta	ek-seen-da
70	evdominta	ev-tho-meen-da
80	ogdónta	og-thon-da
90	eneninta	e-ne-neen-da
100	ekató	e-ka-to
200	diakósia	thya-kos-ya
1,000	chília	cheel-ya
2,000	d'yo chiliádes	thee-o cheel-ya-thes
1,000,000	éna ekatomm'yrio	e-na e-ka-to-mee-ree-o

Time, Days and Months

one minute	éna leptó	e-na lep-to
one hour	mía óra	mee-a o-ra
half an hour	misí óra	mee-see o-ra
quarter of an hour	éna tétarto	e-na te-tar-to
a day	mía méra	mee-a me-ra
a week	mía evdomáda	mee-a ev-tho-ma-tha
a month	énas minas	e-nas mee-nas
a year	énas chrónos	e-nas chro-nos
Monday	Deftéra	thef-te-ra
Tuesday	Tríti	tree-tee
Wednesday	Tetárti	te-tar-tee
Thursday	Pémpti	pemp-tee
Friday	Paraskeví	pa-ras-ke-vee
Saturday	Sávvato	sa-va-to
Sunday	Kyriakí	keer-ee-a-kee
January	Ianouários	ee-a-noo-a-ree-os
February	Fevrouários	fev-roo-a-ree-os
March	Mártios	mar-tee-os
April	Aprílios	a-pree-lee-os
May	Máios	ma-ee-os
June	Ioúnios	ee-oo-nee-os
July	Ioúlios	ee-oo-lee-os
August	Avgoustos	av-goos-tos
September	Septémvrios	sep-tem-vree-os
October	Októvrios	ok-to-vree-os
November	Noémvrios	no-em-vree-os
December	Dekémvrios	de-kem-vree-os

Selected Map Index